Killing The Dream:

America's Flirtation With Third World Status

by

Vern Turner

Table of Contents

Quotes from Famous People

To paraphrase Hermann Goering: *Of course the people don't want a war. But if you keep telling them they are being attacked and that if they don't agree with how the government is handling things you accuse them of being unpatriotic, they'll come along....*

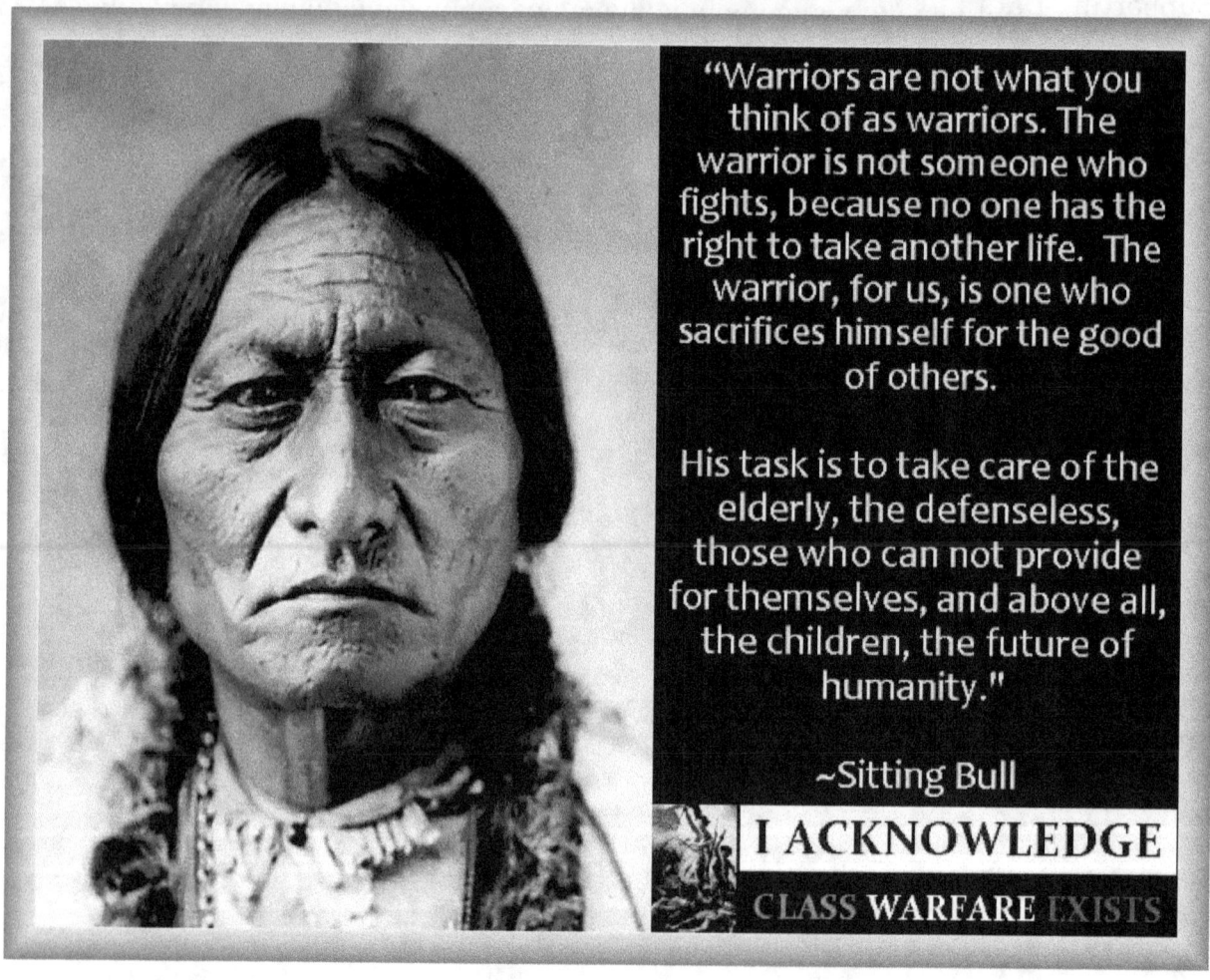

"Warriors are not what you think of as warriors. The warrior is not someone who fights, because no one has the right to take another life. The warrior, for us, is one who sacrifices himself for the good of others.

His task is to take care of the elderly, the defenseless, those who can not provide for themselves, and above all, the children, the future of humanity."

~Sitting Bull

I ACKNOWLEDGE

CLASS WARFARE EXISTS

To laugh often and much; to win the respect of intelligent people and affection of children; to earn the appreciation of honest critics and endure the betrayal of false friends; to appreciate beauty, to find the best in others; to leave the world a bit better, whether by a healthy child or a garden patch or a redeemed social condition; to know even one life has breathed easier because you lived. This is to have succeeded. Ralph Waldo Emerson

Molly Ivins

So keep fightin' for freedom and justice, beloveds, but don't you forget to have fun doin' it. Lord, let your laughter ring forth. Be outrageous, ridicule the fraidy-cats, rejoice in all the oddities that freedom can produce. And when you get through kickin' ass and celebratin' the sheer joy of a good fight, be sure to tell those who come after how much fun it was.

the other 98%

John Kenneth Galbraith

The modern conservative is engaged in one of man's oldest exercises in moral philosophy; that is, the search for a superior moral justification for selfishness.

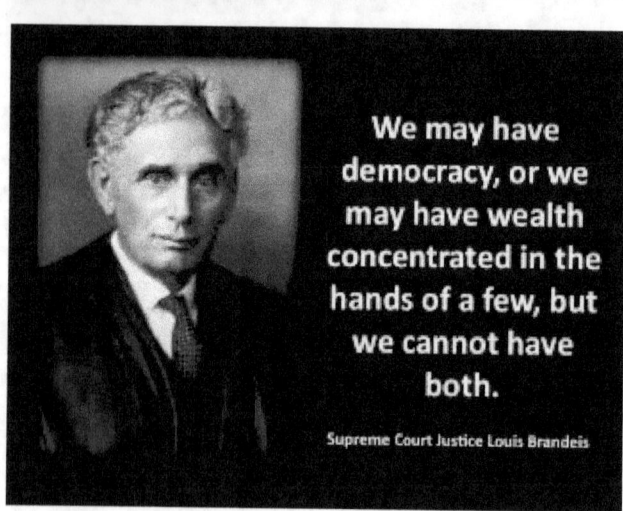

We may have democracy, or we may have wealth concentrated in the hands of a few, but we cannot have both.

Supreme Court Justice Louis Brandeis

There is nobody in this country who got rich on his own. NOBODY.

You built a factory out there -- good for you. But I want to be clear. You moved your goods to market on the roads the rest of us paid for. You hired workers the rest of us paid to educate. You were safe in your factory because of police forces and fire forces that the rest of us paid for. You didn't have to worry that marauding bands would come and seize everything at your factory... Now look. You built a factory and it turned into something terrific or a great idea -- God Bless! Keep a Big Hunk of it. But part of the underlying social contract is you take a hunk of that and pay forward for the next kid who comes along.

- Elizabeth Warren

facebook.com/beingliberal.org

Of course I believe in the free enterprise, but in my system of free enterprise, the Democratic principle is that there never was, never has been, and never will be room for the ruthless exploitation of the many for the benefit of the few.

33.

Harry S. Truman 1945-1953

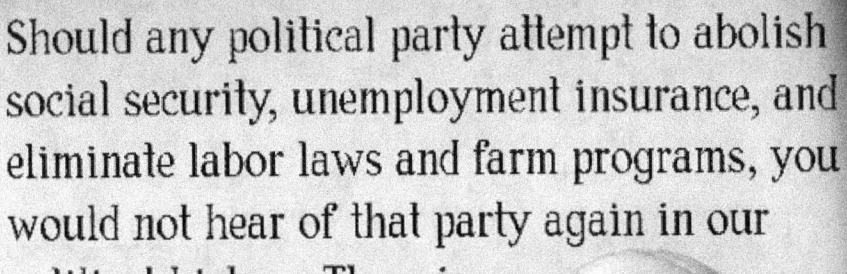

Should any political party attempt to abolish social security, unemployment insurance, and eliminate labor laws and farm programs, you would not hear of that party again in our political history. There is a tiny splinter group, of course, that believes you can do these things. Their number is negligible and they are stupid.

INTRODUCTION

Molly Ivins is one of my literary heroes in that she always seemed to come up with the appropriate nose tweak to the individual who absolutely needed tweaking the most. She and Lou DuBose wrote two books about George W. Bush. They were not complimentary to the man. What caught my eye was something in the second book, *Bushwhacked*. They poked the general public in the eye by saying something like: If you'd read our first book (*Shrub*) about this guy, we wouldn't have had to write this one. In the first book they warned us about the lightness of the being, Bush, and what a terrible thing it would be if he were elected President. In the second book, they showed us how right they were. History corroborated their suspicions and predictions.

My first published book, *The Voter's Guide to National Salvation*, was a compendium of my newspaper columns appearing in *The River Cities Daily Tribune* in Marble Falls, TX. In that first book the subject matter included politics, certainly, but also several pieces on public education and the human propensity to waste things like energy, fuel, food and people. There were even some suggestions about how to fix problems in these areas.

This, my second published book, is similar in construction and subject matter, but also corroborates some predictions and conclusions made in the first one. Sometimes being right is a bitch and not all that much about which to be smug. It's really disappointing, for example, to have predicted a year ago that the onerous decision by the U.S. Supreme Court to give personhood to corporations and unions would create a political horror show that has resulted in the beginnings of a popular movement known as "Occupy". I noted in both books that rubbing the peoples' noses into the arrogance of a corrupt court and government was bound to cause this disturbance that threatens to become a full-blown revolution. The really goofy thing is that it was so unnecessary. Lobbying, aka bribery, was already taking its toll on the moral fiber of our weak-kneed Congress critters at every level by lavishing millions of dollars on them to get votes on laws that suited their sponsors. *Citizens United vs. Federal Election Commission* was overkill and it caused a reaction among the general public – finally.

In reading the published columns and the other essays that needed more than the 700 words allowed by my editor, I hope you will get a better grasp of the issues that are "operating" (or not) our nation and its communities. The main theme is about exercising our right to choose who and what we want to represent us and how we want the money spent to make our communities and country a fine place to live, work, love, learn and recreate.

Enjoy the trip through my tortured mind and soul, but whatever you think of my politics, my opinions, my suggestions and my style, always know that I try to serve the best interests of not only those who think like me, but for the general public who must endure the outcomes of what our governments do and what *we* must do to participate in this great democracy. I am a liberal thinker with progressive ideas because I believe from observation and history that that is the only way to manage a growing country and world population of humans that threatens to extinguish itself by overindulgence, a dearth of understanding about who and what we are, a preoccupation with religious zealotry that is all too often misguided and counterproductive and a propensity for doing harm to one another just for the sake of being able to do so.

In a recent book, *The Watchman's Rattle,* the author, Rebecca Costa discusses memes and "supermemes" by which we operate our societies and cultures. She points out that one of the supermemes, economics, has supplanted humanism as the chief operating philosophy. If what we plan to do doesn't create profit or takes more money than can be immediately seen as a return, it doesn't get done. We no longer seem able to do things just because they are the right thing to do. Everything has to go through a short-term, quarterly financial report filter before it will be implemented. From this position of self-paralysis, it is easy to see how and why the United States has fallen behind the rest of the world in just about every way you can imagine. What is sadly ironic about that is that many of those areas were ones in which we were once the best and set the progressive standard for the rest of the growing world to follow. We were validated by that following even as those countries surpassed us in each area, one by one.

As I've grown older my reading choices have gravitated more toward "what really happened" kind of history rather than the revisionist stuff that keeps finding its way into the media, social networking and magazines specific to a particular time. Howard Zinn's *A People's History of the United State* was a real eye opener for me in that it documented the history of labor as a major theme from the mid-19th century onward. As a result, I got to learn about the history of capitalism and its opposite, communism. (I won't even address socialism at this time, because so many aspects of it are blended into both opposing socio-political systems.) The horrors visited upon the worker by powerful corporations and their remarkably crude management in the early days shook me to my core.

I worked in union and non-union shops as a blue collar worker. I worked as an industrial engineer, representing management to find ways for improving profit and production. I belonged to the *National Education Association* as a school representative. Combining the reading and the work experience, I reached a few conclusions, some of which sound glib, but others quite correct, I think.

- *American workers,* whether or not they are blue or white collar, really don't like to be lumped together. There is that "rugged individualist" in all of us.
- Companies that get unionized, therefore, deserve them. The core tenet of capitalism is to pay the help, a resource, as little as possible to do the most work possible under the most meager conditions they will tolerate.
- *Collective bargaining* is a major part of organized labor because companies know that without labor they have no product. Without product they generate no revenue and no profit. Without profit, the stockholders fire the management, or if it is a private company, the owners sell it to someone who will pay labor what it wants or for what it will negotiate.
- *A living wage* is NOT too much to ask for. A healthy, happy workforce is a highly productive workforce. The trick for both sides is *negotiating* the midpoint where profits are made and workers are compensated such that they can actually buy the products they make. Henry Ford came to that conclusion shortly after perfecting the assembly line and producing more cars than he could sell to rich people.

- *A safe and environmentally sensitive workplace* improves productivity over an unsafe, unhealthy one. Worker fatigue, illness and injury time lost are minimized in a safe, healthy work environment with the associated increase in profit. The data supports this for over 100 years of collecting it.

A populist orator, Mary Elizabeth Lease explained, during the *prairie revolt* that: "Wall Street owns the country...Our laws are the output of a system which clothes rascals in robes and honesty in rags. The political parties lie to us and the political speakers mislead us....money rules!" The year was 1890.

In 1971, Lewis Powell, a corporate lawyer and board member of Philip Morris sent a secret memo around to his pals at the U.S. Chamber of Commerce. In it he promoted a call to arms against anything progressive or even hinting of New Deal thinking. In short, he intended to create a network of conservative action groups to protect the rich from the rabble of labor and especially its unions. He intended to weld corporate financial power with politics. The intent was also to control the media and education to promote a growing plutocracy where the rich and powerful ruled the government, not the other way around, and least of all from having the "common man" actually be represented.

Through the period from 1933 onward FDR's New Deal had sustained its momentum through all the administrations through Lyndon Johnson. Prior to Powell's memo Ralph Nader's activism movement regarding product safety and the environment created a whole new atmosphere among young people such that Congress and even Richard Nixon acted to embrace this new America. Nixon signed into law the *National Environmental Policy Act* and created the *Environmental Protection Agency.* Congress added new parts to the *Clean Air Act* and the EPA introduced the first air pollution standards. There were even new regulations directed at certain pesticides and lead-based paints. Corporate America now saw that they weren't going to have it all their way anymore.

Powell called all this activism an attack on the free enterprise system. He urged corporate America to fight back hard against these new regulations and laws. Among other things, Lewis Powell promoted taking actions to:

- Build a movement.
- Have speakers promote his agenda across the country.
- Attack universities, the media and the courts to cease and desist from these activities.
- Keep TV programming "under constant surveillance".
- Cultivate political power and use it aggressively and without embarrassment among businesses and for the benefit of business.

Powell also thought he could turn the U.S. Chamber of Commerce into a council to combat the activism he saw as a threat to the status quo and his ideas about free enterprise. He thought, though, that business executives had "little stomach for hard-nose contests with their critics" and "little skill in effective intellectual and philosophical debate". He felt they should create think tanks, legal foundations and front groups. We know them today as PACs. In short, Lewis Powell wanted to create a monopoly of monopolies wherein business and corporations of every type would form a united front against the New Deal and progressive ideas in all aspects of American life. The other name for this kind of financial-political front is a *PLUTOCRACY.*

This secretive memo surfaced after Powell was named to the Supreme Court by Nixon. Within two years of its publication, the U.S. Chamber of Commerce had formed a group of 40 business executives from the top corporations in the country including two media giants. Their job was to organize and coordinate the crusade that Powell suggested and put it into effect. The historian Kim Phillips-Fein said, "Many who read (Powell's) the memo cited it afterward as inspiration for their political choices."

It didn't take that long to get started. In 1971 there were only 175 lobbyists in Washington. By 1982 there were 2,500 of them. Corporate political action committees (PACs) rose from fewer than 300 in 1976 to over 1,200 by the mid-80s. Many groups sprung up to provide the philosophical arm of this "revolt of the rich". They included *Business Roundtable,* the *American Legislative Exchange Council (ALEC),* the *Heritage Foundation,* the *Cato Institute,* the *Manhattan Institute* and *Citizens for a Sound Economy* (now called *Americans for Prosperity,* the group sponsored and funded by the Koch brothers). These groups, and others, still exist and exert great influence over how our government works. Many believe that the U.S. Supreme Court's *Citizens United* decision is the culmination of these decades of influence buying and selling because it gives corporations unlimited funding capability for elections and those running for election.

From this time forward people like Nixon's Secretary of the Treasury, William Simon have kept this momentum toward plutocracy going with books and statements that basically say "funds generated by business" must "rush by multimillions" into conservative causes to uproot the institutions and "the heretical strategy" of the New Deal. He called on "men of action in the capitalist world" to start and maintain a "veritable crusade" against progressive America. Can you see and hear the evangelical zeal in words like "heretical" and "crusade"?

Well, here we are in 2011 viewing what all this influence peddling and buying has turned our country into and what the prospects for the short term or long-term future are. Today we see that the rich and the politically powerful have not been content with just being capitalists where they could buy more of everything, but rather as exploiters of what they have done while forever seeming to want more of what everybody else has no matter how little. The operators of this new "Gilded Age" appear to want nothing less than total control over every American life and every American dollar. This "crusade" is in the middle of destroying the middle class and with that the dreams that so-called ordinary Americans have harbored for generations.

By calling the New Deal heretical, the plutocrats and their wannabes have thumbed their noses at anyone who, in their restricted judgment, doesn't earn every penny through labor that enriches *them,* the plutocrats. The unemployment insurance paid from lost jobs belongs to *them.* The health care funding for those who can't afford the outrageous gouging by "private" insurers belongs to *them.* The money spent on educating those children from families who can't afford "private" schools belongs to *them*. The only thing that they don't want for themselves is paying their fair share of taxes to support, expand and rebuild an infrastructure.

This book is about the details of this takeover by the few to control the many. It's not just governing we're talking about here, it is *control*. The plutocrats don't want to just govern; they want to rule by fiat. They want *control* of all the money, just like they did during the early days of the industrial revolution. The New Deal, labor laws, unions and FDR kept them from doing it back then. That is why they must see government programs that actually help working class people as counter to their intentions.

I hate to say it, but Marx and Engels described our current circumstance in the middle of the 19th century. They said that unregulated capitalism will destroy itself from within. How did they know that much about human nature that they saw the green-eyed monster of greed as the great destroyer of great possibilities? Ironically, by trying to gain ALL the wealth, the mechanism for creating wealth, aka labor, will be squeezed into subsistence living and will no longer be the engine that drives progress, innovation and financial success among those who aspire to greatness. No, instead the plutocracy will guarantee mediocrity, an unhealthy populace and an ignorant one to boot. This may present the illusion of having control over the masses, but what it really does is sow the seeds of rebellion and real revolution.

Did you ever stop to wonder why educated, super rich mogul types don't get that? Did they all sleep through *Western Civilization*? Did they all sleep through all their history classes? I think it was the philosopher Santyana who originally said, "Those who fail to learn from the lessons of history are doomed to repeat the mistakes of history".

This book attempts to address the issues, in detail, as they occurred to me during the last two years and to provide some solutions that can save us from the return to the *Middle Ages*. I think that the prospects of serfdom in the coming decades are quite real, and I'm just ornery enough to resist those prospects with as much effort as I have left for as long as I have it. My predecessors worked too hard and sacrificed too much to allow a few hundred spoiled children to run my life or yours, because they will do *their* best to ruin those lives and in so doing, the greatest experiment in democracy the world has ever seen.

I want to be sure to credit Bill Moyers for a speech of great worth from which much of this introduction was taken and modified to fit my own statements.

Why Destroy America?

The history of American capitalism is as long as the country's history; they are intertwined, but very dynamic and ever-changing. American capitalism is theoretically combined with democracy while it embraces a republican form of government: we the people elect representatives to government to fulfill the requirements of the Constitution. This experiment has seen a very uneven evolution from fractured ideals about how laws should be written and enforced to allowing capitalists to exploit resources and people to extremes while building wealth and infrastructure the likes of which the world has never seen.

Some of the trials in this experiment have been bloody, filled with inconceivable graft and greed, ethno-economic strife not even Karl Marx could have predicted and yet retained the ability for the people to close ranks enough during times of acute peril to defeat some of the most dastardly humans and societies that ever walked the Earth. The illusion that our foes of many years, the Soviet Union, would beat us to the moon, thus allowing them to have the "high ground" for military purpose, drove us to fly men to the moon and "return them safely to the Earth."

We now reside in a place in time (2011) when the fabric of this great society's has never been so stretched with internal strife, divisions of purpose, divisions of social class, reluctance to compromise, proponents of hate, media-directed politics and an economic pendulum swing bordering on disaster for not only our country but the world's economy. The battles between labor and business have varied greatly, but continue today as a kind of endless dance of ideologies: fairness vs. profit, or sharing vs. hoarding. These are the seeds of our discontent.

Economics is an abstraction invented by humans in an attempt to remove chaos from ever-growing society-tribes. Bartering or trading of tangible objects began the long trail toward exotic, packaged loans and derivatives we see in today's headlines, documentaries and courts of law. Modern humans understand economics and the rules of supply and demand, markets and even the advanced abstraction of money.

Once money took over as the chief commodity in economics, struggles for obtaining more of it than the next guy became the "normal" way of life among "civilized" nations. Money is used to buy things that previously were bartered for or would still be if there was no money. Now, money has status above anything known before. It is fought over, killed for, counterfeited, stolen and used as a status symbol. It even is the reason for wars between large societies. How it got this way can be included in the discussion about how humans managed to survive at all in a hostile environment with few physical skills and abilities compared to their predators.

Humans became hoarders of food and water so they could have something in "reserve" when the wells dried up or the game became too difficult to follow or catch. When those humans had to travel long distances to follow their food sources they learned to carry reserve sustenance with them along the way. If they didn't start harvesting more food before their cache ran out, they perished. Those that survived were the best at hoarding and storing and rationing their resources. We haven't changed that much over the last 200,000 years, but now money is the resource instead of dried meat and goatskins filled with water...in most places on Earth.

The late Desmond Morris wrote a book called *The Naked Ape.* In it he talked about tribes and super tribes. Today, modern societies can be called not only super tribes, but *Super Duper Tribes.* As opposed to the Neolithic tribes of yore, our modern S-D tribes are all about specialists. Not everyone can perform the majority of the tasks to keep our individual domicile, family, village (tribe) or country (S-D tribe) running smoothly. In short, the S-D tribe's very existence relies on its specialists to provide the environment where economics can be practiced. This arrangement lets almost everyone in advanced societies have enough to eat, shelter, clothing and even an education to provide still more opportunity for specialization. So far, great!

As with ancient times, some of our modern specialists make things for the benefit of most members of their S-D tribe or other tribes that desire the products of those specialists. These specialists get paid in the form of money. Along with the development of the concept of money came the associated concepts of power and control. The modern equation rapidly became established: The more money was relied upon as the tool of barter, the concept of acquiring as much money as possible yielded increased control over the markets, and what the individual could acquire. Soon, labor became a bartered commodity; some people would perform their labor for more or less money depending on what the market would bear for their particular skill. These basic principles of economics are practiced today and the desire for money and its stepchild, power, are taken to extremes both to glorify human achievement as well as to debase human life and dignity to horrific proportions. Slavery, of course, is the ultimate exploitation of human labor.

In the last third of the 20th century, the United States was the pinnacle of all things technological, financial and societal. Oh, there was still that nagging 15% of the citizens who constituted the permanent "underclass" in America, but we charged ahead anyway putting men on the moon for barely more reason than to say we could do it, inventing all sorts of antibiotics to cure diseases around the world - if the infected people or country had enough money to pay for the drugs. Things never looked better during the post-WW II years as employment remained high due to major national projects that paid people sufficiently to buy homes, cars, appliances and clothing without having to go into deep debt. The fuel that drove this economic engine was money....lots of it.

Immediately after the war, the Truman administration was pressured by a republican Congress to cut off lend-lease aid to Europe. Typical of short-sighted, self-absorbed politicians, it was when England and the other devastated nations needed it the most. Despite pleas from the Ambassador to Great Britain Gil Winant and the British government, our Congress just ignored them and went on with the task of filling the international trade void left by the crumbling British Empire. Only later did the great George C. Marshall not only realize that putting Europe back on its feet was beneficial to international trade, but he saw a moral obligation to our allies who also fought and died in the war. Indeed, American casualties were the fewest of any of the participating nations in that war. The American economy was also the only one to enjoy immense prosperity during and after World War II. Once again, though, we see how money clouds judgment even for times when friends helped defeat the tyranny of National Socialism that could have destroyed most of western civilization. The *Marshall Plan* to rebuild Europe and its economies is still at the pinnacle of human altruism and acts as a model for fixing what our own greed, stupidity, hubris and irresponsibility had broken.

The tax rate on the wealthiest Americans at the end of the war was about 90%. That rate stayed near that height up to 1981. Unemployment was very low, there were shallow, short-lived recessions and the growth of the middle class became the driving force that made all businesses flourish. The top tax bracket was reduced to about 70% during the Eisenhower administration and we built the interstate highway system which fueled (pun intended) a second major expansion of motor vehicle travel and the vacation industry to say nothing of reducing interstate commerce costs. This was aided by cheap motor fuels, of course, while the railroads struggled to compete with new shipment philosophies like *Just In Time* where goods no longer languished in warehouses but were shipped virtually factory direct to the points of sale.

Labor unions enjoyed the booming times and negotiated many very high-paying contracts for their employees that included generous retirement and lifetime health care plans during those post-war years. These were the days before Medicare and several other agencies intended to provide a safety net for our hardworking populace. Social Security and unemployment compensation were relatively new ideas implemented since the mid-1930s. The vision of Franklin Roosevelt came true in that a well-paid workforce became the consumer engine that drove successful businesses everywhere. It didn't last and it wasn't utopian by any means, but it demonstrated what is possible when people have freedom from want.

The Republican Party, still smarting from being shut out of the White House and reduced in influence since 1932, harbored great resentment toward progressive programs, labor and how money got distributed among the people. This resentment was driven by corporate and banking America. Banks abhorred the Glass-Steagall Act of 1933 because it prevented them from making speculative investments with depositor money. It also prevented them from insuring themselves against loss from such speculation. These protections were necessary in 1932 and they still are today.

Unfortunately, a republican renaissance occurred during President Clinton's second term that culminated in the repeal of the Glass-Steagall Act in 1999. This terrible decision showed us how craven the money industry was in 2002-2008 when a near international collapse of the global economic system shook the world and threw millions out of work and out of their homes. More on that later...

With the election of Ronald Reagan a system of economics known as *Supply Side Economics* became the meme of Republican politics and their party. This invention of Milton Friedman was intended to have a balanced government budget as its basis. Then, corporations and the highest tax payers were supposed to have their taxes cut (Friedman thought that taxes were socialist and therefore evil) to about half of what they were during

Eisenhower's administration. The theory here was for this extra money among the elites and the rich to "trickle down" to the middle and lower classes by way of capital investment in business thus creating jobs and continued prosperity for all. It didn't work.

It didn't work for three basic reasons. First, government isn't a business. It's a management agency that is committed to serving the people who elected it into being such that the general welfare is attended to and, when needed, major national projects are funded to also generate jobs and new businesses to keep the economic ball rolling. The space program that put men on the moon was one such government sponsored project.

Second, the Republican Party renewed it effort to become the anti-labor party. This enabled businesses to cut or freeze pay and lay off workers at their whim in order to increase profits. Union busting was common while the government looked the other way. Reagan even fired all the air traffic controllers for having the temerity to strike for shorter hours and more pay. The government short-sightedness here failed to take into account worker fatigue factors that made controllers more prone to error. This is a major moment in our country's shift from people to money as the most important part of our society.

Third, the Friedman plan called for greatly reduced government. This meant that many government agencies and departments should be slashed or eliminated so as to help balance the budget even though taxes were reduced, tax loopholes were increased and the burden of paying the nation's bills shifted to the middle classes. The lower classes were, as they always have been by republicans and democrats, ignored. The Reagan administration even wanted to eliminate the Department of Education thus giving the states more control over educating future generations of children as they saw fit.

Well, in order to balance the budget in the face of creating the 600 ship Navy, a Star Wars type missile defense program and a *growing* government payroll, the Reagan administration raised taxes…11 times during his 8 years in office. Ironically, each time the taxes were cut by the government, unemployment went up and more people were paid unemployment support for doing no work. Each time the taxes were increased, unemployment went down, thus adding more taxpayers to the revenue stream. This much documented phenomenon, incredibly, was lost on the "conservative" ideologues who still advocated *Supply Side* disciplines. One of these ideologues was Grover Norquist.

Grover Norquist to this day (2011) continues to trumpet *Supply Side Economics* as the be all and end all of American finance. During the Bush II administration, taxes were cut at the same time we began two misbegotten wars. I skipped over the Bush I presidency not only for its irrelevance but for the fact that Bush I had to raise taxes after promising not to in order to balance the budget. It didn't work then. It also didn't work during Bush II. The increased revenue enjoyed by the beneficiaries of the Bush II tax cuts was funneled into the deregulated banks for hedge fund investments, overseas deposits and a variety of other legal and illegal activities that removed trillions of dollars from the American economy. It was the most affluent Americans who also enjoyed the majority of the tax cuts and the benefits from de-regulated banking.

During this growing financial nightmare, the national money surplus accrued during the 1990s was turned into a $1 trillion deficit in less than 4 years. The nation elected Bush II for the first time in 2004. You will recall that the Supreme Court decided that Bush should be President in 2001 when they denied a counting of ALL the ballots cast in Florida. James Baker, Bush I's former secretary of state was hired by the Bush family to make sure Bush II received a favorable judgment. We saw how well that worked out.

Add to all this, corporate America was allowed to send jobs to other countries because of cheaper labor rates. If a company had union "difficulties", they merely packed up the factory and sent it Mexico, Asia or even Europe. No unions. No problem. More profits. This formula is now an established part of economics in the United States.

There's more: During the Bush II years, government regulatory agencies were cut completely, or their budgets reduced by huge percentages. This allowed below standard imports of everything including drugs and children's' goods to enter our environment. Tainted food imported or from now un-inspected domestic processing plants also entered into the American product stream. Pollution controls were either ignored or diluted. Companies were asked to "voluntarily" implement environmental controls over their pollution by-products. This was done in the spirit of smaller government at the same time the Department of Homeland Security was invented and funded to the tune of $500 billion. The government payroll increased by 40,000 jobs in the security sector while budgets and jobs in those sectors that directly benefited ordinary citizens were cut during the years 2001-2008. The Bush II administration thwarted Medicare from negotiating best prices from drug companies and created Medicare Part D that allows pharmaceutical companies to charge the government any amount it wants. This money, of course, comes from the tax payer. Rigged systems like this used to be called rackets.

These and other fear-based actions were predicated on the 11 September 2001 attacks that generated the hastily produced *Patriot Act.* This piece of legislation basically neutralized the 4th amendment to the U.S. Constitution protecting its citizens from unwarranted search and seizure by government agents. The attorney general at this time was John Ashcroft from Missouri. He was the man who lost an election to someone who died during the campaign. So, Bush II picked him to be attorney general. Of course...

If you have slogged through this history lesson, you might be wondering about the good news. As of this writing, there isn't much to brighten our days as a nation. Our founding fathers are being touted by some, then ignored and misinterpreted. Our financial apparatus continues to sell packaged loans and operate as if the economic crisis never happened. Grover Norquist has "demanded" that Republican Congress people sign a pledge that they will never, ever vote for increased taxes on anything, thus cutting off revenue growth in order to pay off the now growing $15 trillion deficit. Furthermore, our "representatives" in government are almost all millionaires and have to campaign and fund raise more than they actually perform in office.

The conclusion to this review of events starts with the question: Why do so many people with so much money want to destroy the very entity that not only allowed them to become so rich and powerful, but if managed correctly would continue to do so for the foreseeable future? How do corporate moguls justify sending millions of U.S. dollars and jobs overseas, then have the temerity to complain about having to pay too much in taxes? Well, to their "credit", they convinced enough Congress people to allow them to hide their profits overseas so they wouldn't have to pay taxes on them. They've convinced enough congress people to allow them to claim no regular income, but instead lets them live on *capital gains* that are, unbelievably, taxed at a lower rate than regular income.

How can corporate giants like *General Electric* pay NO taxes? How do they get away with leaving all their profits in Swiss banks earning interest while our citizens run out of unemployment insurance, lose their homes due to being sold bad loans, lose their health care, their pensions and their ability to support their families? How does all this help the United State be great?

The answer is: None of it. Foolishly, the rich have become the power that wags the dog of the government so they can show ordinary people like me that they intend to re-create feudalism within our borders and in our time. This is politely called a *plutocracy*. Is this what *"We the People..."* want? Have any of those wealthy (some would say greedy) people ever grasped the psychology of their own actions and behaviors? How have they managed to avoid most accepted moral and ethical codes to expand their own enrichment while those who helped enrich them are left destitute? Why has the economics meme overtaken doing what is right instead of what is profitable?

The next question is: Does anyone see a final consequence to the collapse or destruction of the United States? Is the rest of the world up to the task of filling the economic void when the U.S. collapses? What passes for our Congress seemed willing to let collapse happen by rejecting a debt ceiling adjustment. Does the rest of the world realize how close they came to having the entire economic and financial universe come apart at the seams because a few politicians decided to behave childishly and ignorantly? Were they practicing the ultimate game of chicken with the other 7 billion people on Earth, or was it just a new way to define hubris? What will these rich moguls do when the goose they created stops laying golden eggs because they didn't feed it? Do they think, really, that their wealth can grow in perpetuity without taking care of that which makes it grow? Has money become more of a tangible part of their psychology than the abstraction it really is?

People much smarter than me have begun to call for a Constitutional amendment that addresses the cause of the problems mentioned above. There is a movement to begin removing corporations and banks from our election process. Their money is an unfair advantage and they can literally bribe their way into our government. The law allows them to do that. In December, 2010, the U.S. Supreme Court made the decision to allow corporations to have equal status as an individual. That meant that a corporation could donate as much money as they liked to any candidate or political party they chose without telling anybody. The recent emergence of political action committees (PACs) is clear evidence as to where this is going. For decades lobbyists have been bribing politicians to do the bidding of those they, the lobbyists, represent. How can that be fair to the general citizenry? It cannot.

We are about to find out what we're made of as citizens. We may have to do things we haven't done since the 18th century to save our nation from our internal enemies, the enemies who want to destroy our country for their own wealth and power. History from medieval Europe has shown us how well that works. Revolutions are fought to eliminate those lusting for power and who do so irrespective of the law. Eras have died and been born over these issues throughout the history of western civilization. Is this our turn? Is it now up to us to get our hallowed document changed such that it serves the people it was intended to serve and allows us once again to elect representatives that represent the citizen in general rather than the richest among us?

Personally, I do not choose to be a serf. I choose to defend the Constitution against all enemies, foreign and domestic. I choose to advocate for whatever action is required to get the amendment written and passed and implemented in order to save American citizens from those who can't control their greed, who've abdicated their morals and ethics to the abstraction called money and from those who think that war is the answer to all disagreements. How smart are we? Will it be a peaceful exercise, or will the powerful unleash their employees against the will of the people? We'll soon see.

A Meaningful Lesson in History-Part I

My wife and I treated ourselves to a winter holiday gift by traveling to London, England. We arrived on Christmas morning, a chilly, drippy day, but while riding to our hotel we noticed people queuing up at churches along the 18 mile route from Heathrow airport. Having visited England during this season before, I knew that most Britons attend midnight services on Christmas Eve. Seeing these churchgoers in the late morning told me they still care about their religion and faith.

After settling in at the hotel, we strolled toward Westminster Palace, the seat of government. My wife had never been to London, so I just kept quiet while the twin steeples of Westminster Abbey crept into view from around a corner on Victoria Street. Again, there were many people trying to enter for their P.M. services even though the "museum" part of the church was closed.

The museums and galleries were closed on Christmas and Sunday, the 26th (Boxing Day, or St. Stephen's Day), so we took a river cruise along the Thames all the way to Greenwich where I straddled the prime meridian; another check on my "bucket list". It was a partly sunny day and we thoroughly enjoyed the sites and guided narrative.

Major museum and area highlights included Kew Royal Botanical Gardens, the RAF museum, the British Museum of Natural History (One of the most beautiful buildings in the world, in my opinion), the Victoria & Albert museum (3 floors of exquisite art from cultures around the world), the Tower of London and the Science museum. Seeing *The Nutcracker* ballet at the Coliseum Theater was stunning. We took a day trip to Windsor Castle, Stonehenge and Oxford. Walks around town included Hyde Park and the attendant monuments and places of government; the variation in architecture was mind-boggling while some of the buildings and statues simply oozed with history.

What struck me most during the long plane ride home was the utter volume of things, discoveries and events that spilled over their shores to ours for nearly the last 400 years. Added to that the awe-inspiring experience of seeing original masterpieces from the likes of van Dyke, Rembrandt, Turner (no relation), Gaugin and van Gogh just to name a few, gave me better appreciation for the creative mind of man over such a long time.

The Science museum exhibited the evolution of industrial engines since the first one built in the 18th century to pull water out of coal mines in Wales. It bore a striking resemblance to our lever-action oil rigs here in Texas. The wing dedicated to ships displayed the entire history of boats, ships and the means that powered them; wind, oar or engine. There were dozens of ship engine models placed near ship models that used them. The same organization described the "Flight" wing: Original early fliers and gliders pre- and post-dating the Wright Brothers' machine, aircraft engines from the first low horsepower versions to modern fan jets that flew us to and from England.

Then there was the history of politics, kings, queens and the bloody, bloody events that kept fertilizing the soil of Great Britain. From Windsor Castle to the Tower, we saw over-the-top opulence juxtaposed against medieval weaponry and what passed for justice before and after the invention of a parliamentary form of government. Similar to our government's behavior these days, their kings and Prime Ministers fought with the parliament over everything, but mostly about power.

There is a sculpted crystal pillow on the grounds of the Tower that consecrated the site for heads being rolled in centuries past. Today, death penalties are doled out much more parsimoniously in Western civilization. Back then, one lost his/her head (think: Ann Bolyn for not being able to produce a viable male heir for Henry VIII) for things other than murder or treason.

There are those self-ordained experts in this country who sneer and look down their noses at British/European history and government. None of it is perfect. But since the Norman conquest of 1066 A.D. and the signing of the *Magna Carta* in 1215 by King John, continued efforts toward perfecting Constitutional law have driven Western civilization onward. That is called PROGRESS.

Will Hate Media Destroy our Freedoms?

The current debate raging among pundits, politicians and bloggers about how much the vitriolic media environment influenced Jared Loughner or influences any other fringe-of-sanity people is, in my opinion, long overdue. Looking back at some of my columns from last year I saw where I had addressed the hate radio/TV types who continue to use and abuse their first amendment rights to pump up listener ratings.

I read a blog that stated that loudmouths like Rush Limbaugh depend as much on those who despise them as their "faithful" followers. Cynicism doesn't get any more bitter than that. The depravity of this practice transcends all reason and responsibility when it pushes unstable people into doing irrational things. Screamers and hate mongers like Limbaugh, Beck, Hannity, O'Reilly, and Coulter, goad marginal thinkers like Palin, Bachmann, Gingrich, Angles and lesser known political wannabes into thinking they too can capitalize on over the top emotional rhetoric to garner attention, votes and, most importantly, money. These creatures of the dark side are making pots of money on books and TV appearances, while teachers go begging.

When did this all become so insane? I'm suggesting that this "style" of politics began with the emergence of the Karl Rove philosophy of scorched earth, attack dog methods to alienate and divide an electorate without the benefit of intelligent or mature discourse. In Rove's world, the candidate never admitted a mistake, blamed everybody else for his/her own screw ups and attacked the character and persona of the opponent irrespective of facts or truth. Creating scandal for the sake of scandal was strategy #1 for this method of electioneering.

Karl Rove was hired by George H.W. Bush to run his election campaigns because he saw that Rove's methods worked. He took it to a national level when Poppy ran against St. Ronald in Republican primaries. Where do you think the term "Voodoo Economics" came from? Bush ran on that phrase until he realized that he was going to lose and the only way to salvage his political career was to toady-up and get himself selected as V.P. to the sainted one.

When Bush ran against Michael Dukakis, Rove kicked things into high gear and, along with Dukakis's own mistakes, overcame a double-digit lead and helped get Bush elected. The Willy Horton mess was typical Rove. It had no relevance whatsoever to the election, but it was presented in such a way as to sink Dukakis's campaign. That was just the beginning.

You may be thinking back to Nixon's "dirty tricks" team back in the 70s, but that was just Karl Rove's graduate course in divisive politics. After Bush lost to Clinton in 1992, the gloves really came off. Clinton's hand wasn't even off the Bible before the hate and scandal campaign against him began. Even the conservative, erudite pundit George Will was shocked at the depth and viciousness of those attacks.

About this time the opportunist, Rush Limbaugh, saw ways to make lots of money by thumping the hate card with half-truths, outright lies and opinions that would have made Joseph Goebbels blush. He became highly successful at this "act" eventually signing long-term radio contracts worth upwards of $40 million per year.

Limbaugh became the archetype for anger baiting programming. Following his obvious success, Fox Broadcasting, led by the discredited Australian, Rupert Murdoch, hired Roger Ailes to lead the news sections. Ailes worked for Rove in the Bush campaigns and wrote some of Bush's most disturbing speeches. Ailes hired O'Reilly, Beck, Hannity and a research staff dedicated to demonizing anything more liberal than the script of the RNC and Murdoch.

To me, this use of mass communications for the specific purpose of enraging a poorly informed populace to elect their selected candidates violates every particle of ethics and responsibility by those media. Maybe Loughner wasn't pushed to his killing frenzy by hate radio, but somebody might; somebody who is less able to resist the gut-wrenching vitriol coming from right wing political activism.

The multiple facts of extremist propaganda, readily available weapons, a poorly informed populace, anger/hate mongering politicians and the number of mentally unstable people walking the streets could create the perfect storm for more political assassination attempts the likes of which we haven't seen in this country – ever.

A Meaningful Lesson in History-Part II

One of the most intriguing visits I made while in London, England was to Westminster Abbey. Many famous Britons from all fields of endeavor are entombed there. Many of these tombstones have been trod upon for so long that the carved inscriptions are barely readable.

Three tombs especially interested me and were placed within a few paces of one another. Isaac Newton, Charles Lyell and Charles Darwin together form the core of modern scientific thinking.

Newton is famous for his laws of physics wherein he predicted in the 17th century that if an object had enough velocity it could escape the pull of Earth's gravity. This little tidbit was a result of him formulating the force of gravity on all matter. By the way, he also invented Calculus, the mathematical tool that allowed 20th century man to figure out how to send somebody to the moon...among other things.

Charles Lyell is not as well known as the other two, but all their work and writings are linked for all time. Lyell, in the 19th century was the first scientist to determine that the Earth was significantly older than what the Church of England dictated. His discoveries of fossils of organisms that no longer existed led him to postulate that some rocks were not always rocks. As a result of this and other work with the ground in England and Scotland, he is known as the *Father of Geology.*

Charles Darwin, and his contemporary, Alfred R. Wallace, wrote from their experiences in the far corners of the world as the first true naturalists to step out of the "creationist" box. They determined that organisms changed over time and that new forms of life were constantly appearing and old ones disappearing for reasons of adaptability to their environments. Their theoretical work of the 19th century led to the melding of modern genetics and biology to geology. This relationship now explains how the Earth and its living things came to be and continue to change. Some call evolution a theory, but it is only theoretical in the sense of not being able to see HOW life and land changed on Earth over billions of years. The facts are that those changes indeed occurred.

Another outcome of my recent visit to England was the relative ease of transfer of science and government between that country and ours. One of the most vexing of these is the *welfare* or *nanny* state. Great Britain saw the value of tending to its needy citizens and providing all with at least a solid education in those subjects needed for either higher education or the trades. But as with our welfare systems instituted in the 1960s, proper oversight of these bureaucracies went glimmering for the sake of fiscal restraint. Big mistake...

Human nature pushes us to find the easiest path to our own survival. If it's easier to take a handout than work, pride goes out the window and the "dole" becomes the norm. That is the case in Britain and that is what we struggle with here. We didn't learn from their mistakes.

Bill Clinton instituted *workfare* in the 90s to get people trained to work and off of welfare. It worked. Then, the next administration canceled the program because it was....well, Clinton's.

Similarly, however, the term *socialized medicine* is a canard thrown out by conservatives in this country to make sure health care insurance companies make their profits off the sick.

In Britain, government-sponsored, single-payer health care works. It may not be ideal, but the WHO statistics show that Britons are generally healthier than their American counterparts by large margins. Britons also have the right to (a) buy their own health care insurance and (b) see physicians of their choice irrespective of how their needs are served. Our new House speaker is telling us they want to "repeal" the health care reform laws (even before they've been implemented) because it kills jobs. Huh?!

If you really want to kill jobs have a sick workforce. Healthy workers are productive and pay taxes. The only jobs being killed are those from the medical insurers who charge between 30%-60% above the cost of care for their "administrative costs" and profit. If a country has confidence that its physicians are competent, why pay a for-profit middleman?

The Symptoms of Disease

We all know that doctors who treat symptoms rather than causes of disease are not doing their best jobs. It's their job to take the symptoms we report and they observe and deduce the malady that needs curing. The vast majority of our doctors do their jobs very well. In theory, they are *not* in competition with one another; rather they are doing the right thing by us. In other words, we don't go shopping for the doctor who will cure us, we expect them ALL to be able to cure our health problems: Our health is our expected right when we go to our doctor, not a commodity.

The other item that is clearly NOT a commodity is our children's education. I've often asked, "Why in the world would we want schools to be competitive in the classroom? Why should some of our children be in 'loser' schools while others are in 'winners'? Winners of what?" Shouldn't all our children have the right to a world class education like the one idealized by Thomas Jefferson? Oh. Wait. Cynthia Dunbar, the Virginia-bred stealth member of the Texas state school board says, "No" to Thomas Jefferson. She and the other "conservative" members of the state school board are in the process of writing *revisionist history and economics* for our children. Like they know what they're talking about....

This current school board exhibits symptoms of a growing disease in Texas' state's politics: the disease of ultra-conservatism. When a political entity tries to turn back the clock to a time that never was, that's called backwardness. The agenda-driven movement to destroy reason, fact and truth in our textbooks and in our classrooms is afoot and gaining ground on the rest of us who quaintly cling to our ideals of reason, fact and truth. This school board will be the first to wail about "activist judges" or "revisionist historians" while they hypocritically judge and revise their ways to *their* personal beliefs as part of the curriculum in our schools. In case you forgot, beliefs are not reason, fact or truth; they are a construct of one's own experience and thought. Giving the board the benefit of the doubt, their "thoughts" are arrogant, self-serving and disturbingly one-sided and slanted toward theocratic oligarchy, you know, like they have in Iran.

Don McLeroy, Cynthia Dunbar, Ken Mercer and the rest of the "conservative" bloc on the Texas state school board have already diluted science to the point of absurdity. Thankfully, Dunbar is headed back to Falwell-land and McLeroy was defeated in the primary. That leaves Mercer as the main purveyor of nonsense.

Science teaching doesn't occur without facts. Facts are real, not discussion points. Theories are based on facts, not what-if scenarios. The scientific method is a method of proofs; proofs derived from facts, not mythological discussions of "beliefs". The belief stuff belongs in philosophy classes, not science classes. This issue is a particularly knotty symptom of the ultra-conservative disease spreading throughout our state's education system. Theological issues belong in churches, not our schools. If people are unhappy with their church, they can change churches. Our public schools are not the place for religious instruction as they cannot support all the "beliefs" associated with the widely variable religious entities, especially on the public tax dollar. That's why the Supreme Court has ruled for separating church from state; they want to be fair to the freedom of and from religion, not restrictive of it. Of course, that fact is something of an intellectual leap for some members of state school boards across the country.

So, who is going to be the doctor to cure this disease? Who will prescribe the cure for the malady of agenda-driven public office? What will be the medicine for removing dangerously uninformed people from sensitive positions in government so that our children can flourish in an environment of exploration, truth and security in knowing that what they are reading and learning is not somebody's idea of how things should have been, but how they actually were and are. The doctor is us: You and me. We're the ones who have to return sanity to the process of educating our children. The current regime on the Texas state school board simply cannot be allowed to further destroy the quality of our public education that is already one of the weakest in the nation. We must elect real thinking, caring and honest members to help bring Texas's education to a much higher, healthier place.

UPDATE: Ken Mercer was reelected by a 2:1 margin and the revisionist history, excluding references to Thomas Jefferson other than being the third President, were implemented.

Facts, History and Reality

I am especially gratified to see that Gabrielle Giffords is making such a rapid recovery from being the victim of an assassin's bullet. We can only hope that her recovery progresses such that she is able to return to work as a voice of reason in the Arizona delegation to Congress. It seems, however, that not all Americans share the dramatic events of Tucson as a reflection on certain elements of our society and how large a part guns play in the national psyche.

It didn't take Glenn Beck long, for example, to start talking about shooting people in the head or the forehead. I know there are those who are convinced that Mr. Beck speaks metaphorically about everything and that his "shoot them in the head" rhetoric is a metaphor for something else. I'm not the smartest or the dumbest guy in the world, but I can't figure out how one makes a metaphor of a direct request to shoot "them" in the head. If that is a metaphor, then Mr. Beck is an electronic hologram and doesn't really exist. Maybe that would be better for all of us.

Speaking of loosely-wrapped minds operating a tongue, I couldn't help but wonder what country Michelle Bachmann (R-MN) was talking about when she mentioned in Iowa that our founding fathers tried to abolish slavery. Additionally, her display of remarkably inaccurate graphics during the rebuttal of State of the Union was so obviously biased and un-historic that they were laughable, except nobody was laughing.

Before the Bachmann bit we had the "official" republican response to the President's speech from Paul Ryan (R-WIS). His misrepresentation of the President's work and policies were also blatantly wrong and misleading.

For anyone paying attention, the Bush administration handed off the stimulus work to the Obama administration whereupon it was implemented to stop the hemorrhage of jobs. It worked despite the inputs from professional economists that said that $750 billion was not sufficient to do the job. Well, 2 years later we still haven't spent all that money and job losses have slowed while employment and GDP growth has improved almost every month since.

Furthermore, the bailout of General Motors worked. Just this week (1/24-2011) the *Wall Street Journal* told us that GM showed a profit of $4.2 billion for the past 9 months. They have paid back a significant part of their loan with expectations of paying it all back in the foreseeable future.

Add to that the fact that the bank bailout loans are almost paid back **with interest** such that the government will make money on the deal. I'd say that isn't too bad for a "failed economic plan". When one considers how very close the world was to complete financial collapse, we should be thankful that we had a steady hand on the tiller of the nation and that we could afford to do the things we did to prevent it.

House Speaker John Boehner chipped in with disparaging commentary about the President omitting language about America's exceptional nature. I guess he nodded off when Obama mentioned that at length in two or three different contexts. It was also in the written version of the speech.

Then there is Sarah Palin. Once again she launched into a diatribe of incomprehensible comments and statements that rewrites American history, both past and present, complains about being picked on by those who are making her rich (the press) and has a "WTF" moment of her own by accusing the President of having one. President Obama didn't say it, she did.

The question is, "Is this the best the Tea Party can produce as their front people?" Are there no other members of this now validated movement who can voice a coherent message? I heard some pundits say that republicans are fearful of Palin and Bachmann because their supporters will attack them if they criticize Palin and Bachmann. I guess this all speaks volumes about how deep the republican bench is with ideas and viable national candidates.

My fellow progressives and I will look forward to the next six years of the Obama administration. We will fix the problems created from the previous administration, get our country working again, return it to fiscal soundness and allow us to once again be a world leader in education and healthy citizens.

Statesmanship and American Politics

After the November, 2010 elections I wrote a piece concerning what the newly elected officials would do with their power and influence. Sadly, I was correct in my predictions. So far, it's been posturing and preening and doing things that have virtually nothing to do with the welfare of the people they are supposed to represent, indeed, in their zeal to give the illusion of doing something they have promoted legislation and ideas that are COUNTER-productive to outcomes that benefit most citizens.

The essence of the problem is described quite ably by my colleague Allen Laughlin (The River Cities Daily Tribune) in his column from last week:

I said to my students that the men responsible for creating this great country were not politicians, but statesmen in every sense of the word. They had everything to lose, including their lives, for a belief in liberty.

Today's power-hungry, self-interested politicians pale in comparison, as they pass out our tax dollars to various connected constituencies under the mistaken belief that only they know what is best for us.

The republicans went into office in January with trumpets blaring and flags waving promising to do everything to get America moving again; create jobs, jobs, jobs and reduce the size of government. Well, here are the bills our House of Representatives in Washington with their new collection of Republicans and Tea Partiers has presented so far:

- 16 bills to repeal all or parts of the Affordable Care Act
- 7 bills/resolutions to require a balanced federal budget
- 5 bills to repeal the estate tax (which benefits only the super-wealthy)
- A bill to repeal Wall Street Reform
- 6 bills to restrict women's access to abortions
- A bill to take polar bears off the Endangered Species list
- A bill to pull federal funding of public radio
- Six bills and a resolution to increase oil drilling in the US and to prevent federal regulation of greenhouse gases
- A bill to remove certain Federal restrictions on interstate firearms transactions
- A bill to prohibit paying salaries of "czars" and a resolution that they should be required to get Congressional approval
- A bill to prevent US-born children of undocumented immigrants from being designated as U.S. citizens
- A bill to allow employers that provide health insurance to count that toward their minimum wage compensation
- A bill to prevent the federal government from regulating the internet
- A bill to *permanently* reduce individual income tax rates
- A bill to require States' approval of national monument creation in their state
- A bill to require the heads of all four branches of the military to sign off on DADT before it can be implemented

- A bill to rename two buildings after Presidents George H.W. Bush and George W. Bush
- A bill to require that Gitmo be kept open and that only military commissions be used to try the inmates held there
- A bill to prevent the posting of signs indicating work being done/paid for under the Recovery Act
- A resolution to repeal the 16th Amendment

I ask: "When will you be sponsoring a jobs bill?"

Republicans have been hammering the democrats and President Obama for the past two years about jobs and the economy. You would think they'd be ready to promote their job-creating agenda from the start. But, as you can see, they have *other* priorities.

The Texas governor just gave the *State of the State* address where he extolled the virtues of what passes for conservative politics here while shaking his verbal fist at our federal government. From one fork of his tongue he tells us how great the country is and how proud we Texans are to be part of it. On the other fork he rails at Washington for trying to enforce its laws that the Constitution says states must abide by.

As Mr. Laughlin suggests, these behaviors are not the work of statesmen. It is the work of political hacks elected by a tiny fraction of the people who vote for them. Until a super-majority of our eligible citizens get out and vote, we can expect more of this rubbish, if not worse.

Cuts Making Last Place Worse

To the relief of many readers I am not a native Texan. But that does not exclude me from paying attention. I live here and enjoy the hill country life style immensely. That said I also want to announce that I am proud of where I live and with whom I interact. In fact, I am so enthused about living in Texas that I am highly motivated to point out to my fellow Texas residents and natives that our elected and appointed leaders are making a mockery of our state in just about every way imaginable.

Below is a summary of our ranking among the fifty states in a variety of categories:
Texas' superlatives are nothing to brag about, according to the fifth edition of "Texas on the Brink," summarized by Emily Ramshaw, an annual review that ranks the state on dozens of factors ranging from health insurance to voter turnout.

Despite having the highest birth rate, Texas has the worst rate of women with health insurance, and the worst rate of pregnant women receiving prenatal care in the first trimester, according to the report commissioned by the Legislative Study Group, a research caucus in the Texas House. While Texas has the second-highest public school enrollment, the state ranks last in the percentage of people 25 and older with a high school diploma. And though Texas has the highest percent of its population without health insurance, the state is 49th in per capita spending on Medicaid, and dead last in per capita spending on mental health, according to the report.

Here's a look at how Texas compares to other states:

- *Tax expenditures per capita (47th)*
- *Percent of population 25 and older with a high school diploma (50th)*
- *Percent of poor people covered by Medicaid (49th)*
- *Percent of population with employer-based health insurance (48th)*
- *Per capita spending on mental health (50th)*
- *Per capita spending on Medicaid (49th)*
- *Percent of non-elderly women with health insurance (50th)*
- *Percent of women receiving prenatal care in first trimester (50th)*
- *Average credit score (49th)*
- *Workers' compensation coverage (50th)*
- *Number of executions (1st)*
- *Public school enrollment (2nd)*
- *Percent of uninsured children (1st)*
- *Percent of children living in poverty (4th)*
- *Percent of population uninsured (1st)*
- *Percent of population living below poverty (4th)*
- *Percent of population with food insecurity (2nd)*
- *Overall birth rate (2nd)*
- *Amount of carbon dioxide emissions (1st)*
- *Amount of toxic chemicals released into water (1st)*
- *Amount of hazardous waste generated (1st)*

It doesn't take a genius to see which "brink" they're talking about. What was implied but not listed is Texas' bottom five ranking in secondary school national tests. This begins to gall me when I hear "...great state of Texas..." emitting from politicians. Sorry about the negativity, but waking up to real problems is the first step in fixing them.

Why is our legislature trying to cut even more social services when we're already last? Why is our legislature trying to cut public education funding when we're already last? Why does our legislature and governor refuse federal money for education or refuse federal law to improve our rates of pollution when we're last? Why don't Texans want to pay for anything that benefits the people of the state, the state's ability to compete for high quality businesses, the quality of educating its children, or cleaning up its polluting industries?

Last November the state's voters who turned out elected many republicans who now think they have a mandate to cut waste and bureaucracies. Well, Rick Perry received about 55% of the vote from only 48% of the registered voters who voted. Thirty percent of our eligible voters are not registered. That means that 17% of the people of Texas voted for Rick Perry. It also means that only 24% of those registered to vote voted for him. Does anybody out there not breathing helium see this as a mandate to further worsen our state?

Our state's return to greatness will not happen until its citizens assume responsibility for its government and its social obligation to pay for the services the majority of its people deserve and need.

A Little Nostalgia...

Depending on which day I go shopping for groceries at our local supermarket, I am greeted by one of the musical themes with which I literally grew up. Some days it's the early '50s, the early days of OUR music. Others progress through the British invasion, soul, Motown, folk, harder rock and the terrific musicality of the '70s and '80s. It must seem funny to today's kids seeing all these gray-haired and limping shoppers bobbing their heads to *The Temptations* singing *My Girl*, or singing along to Bob Dylan's *The Times They are a'Changin'*.

I grew up in and around Cleveland, Ohio in the '40s, '50s and '60s. I KNOW why the *Rock and Roll Hall of Fame* was built there. I saw and listened to the cornerstones of the genre being laid every day on the radio and in the record shops. Ah, the record shops... We could go in and select demo records and listen to them in little audio booths before we bought them. That certainly helped separate the junk from the good stuff for each of us.

The radio innovator Alan Freed came to Cleveland from New York and started playing "alternative" pop music. We know this music today as R & B (rhythm and blues). But the real designation was *Real Black*. Thus ensued the battle between my generation of white kids and our parents. Our parents didn't want us to have anything to do with "those" people or "that" music. They didn't use "those" or "that" when searching for adjectives. We, of course, rebelled. We became the James Dean, *Rebel Without a Cause* generation. The "cause" came later.

Mr. Freed became very popular with his "Moondog" radio show that came on around 11:00 P.M. Most of us hid our radios under our pillows to listen to it without the parents interfering with what was rapidly becoming rock and roll. By the way, legend has it that Alan Freed coined that phrase at Elvis Presley's breakout concert at the LaSalle Theatre on Superior Avenue near Case-Western Reserve University in Cleveland. He wrote a review that said something like, "That kid Presley had the old LaSalle rockin' and rollin'."... or so goes the legend.

Alan Freed also organized and held the first rock and roll concert in the Cleveland Arena in 1952. It was a huge hit with kids, but about half-way through it the police came and shut it down. It was simply too much too soon for the ruling generation. We knew, however, that the change was coming and rock and roll music was our vehicle for generation identity and our message for the future.

The first *rhythm and blues* record that made the charts was made by none other than Antoine "Fats" Domino in 1949. *The Fat Man* kicked off a transit of this very rhythmic music up from New Orleans past the Mississippi delta region where it received another blues injection. From the Deep South the music kept traveling north past St. Louis, Missouri where a country kid who "could play a guitar just like ringin' a bell", wrote 36 songs that found their way into every rock and roll hit for the next 40 years.

Chuck Berry's sound enthralled every "sweet li'l sixteen" from Bangor to L.A. and the movement became unstoppable. The rust belt cities of Chicago, Detroit and Cleveland all became hubs for the growth and development of early rock music and artists before it went to New York and became THE musical expression of the late '50s and beyond.

But down in Memphis a branch of this budding genre got "Hill Billied" by not only white musicians but black as well until there was hardly a distinction. *Stax, Sun, Atlantic* and eventually *Motown* became the record labels that produced all the songs from all the people who became the permanent "guests" of that museum up on the shores of Lake Erie.

The best part of this walk of nostalgia for me reminds me how my generation broke down racial and discrimination boundaries that had existed for over a century. We DID it! It is our gift to subsequent generations to keep doing it for the sake of ALL the people of our nation.

Thoughts and Facts Replacing Lies and Fears

Here is a list of victories by working people that are under attack by republicans in the Congress in Washington and in republican dominated state governments. As you listen to the demonization of progressives and liberal thinkers by vacuous vessels like Michelle Bachmann, Rick Perry, John Boehner and the Republican Party's leadership, keep in mind what liberals and unions fought for and earned these benefits most of us now take for granted:

- *The 8 hour work day;*
- *paid holidays;*
- *paid vacations;*
- *sick pay;*
- *pensions;*
- *employer assisted medical insurance;*
- *workplace safety;*
- *Social Security;*
- *Medicare;*
- *The GI Bill;*
- *Consumer Product Safety Commission;*
- *student loans and grants for college;*
- *agencies for ensuring safety in food, water, drugs, toys, automobiles and clothing;*
- *agencies for ensuring clean air to breath and clean water to drink or to recreate;*
- *free public education.*

There has always been feverish opposition to Social Security from republicans. What is happening now, in a period of deficit hysteria, is that this crucial retirement program is being dishonestly lumped together with Medicare as an entitlement program that is driving federal deficits. This is another obvious distortion of truth. In 2000 our government had a budget *surplus* of almost $200 billion. I don't understand why that isn't remembered or how it came to be in view of our fiscal history. A surplus is a rare event. But the republicans do not want to remind us that when they controlled Congress, the White House and most of the Supreme Court, that surplus disappeared in the form of tax cuts for the wealthy and the borrowing of obscene amounts of money for wars of choice.

PEOPLE! We simply cannot forget what caused the problem if we are going to fix it.

The drivers of our deficit are not social programs, even with the expenses of Medicare. Rather they are tax expenditures - to corporations and the wealthy - and our obscene expenditures on the military and our unnecessary expenditures especially in Iraq and Afghanistan, to say nothing of the many billions spent on "intelligence" activities hidden from view and military/ paramilitary operations in hundreds of nations. The country is drowning in a sea of debt because of the obscene Bush tax cuts for the rich, the wars in Afghanistan and Iraq that have never been paid for, the great giveaway to drug companies and the Great Recession.

Republicans insist that the infrastructure rebuilding they opposed (while trying to get pork projects for their districts and states then falsely taking credit when the Federal funds arrived) had to be paid for, even though dedicating current tax revenues to such efforts undermined the overall stimulus effects.

Now some republicans want schools to return the portions of ARRA funding used to keep teachers employed! Of course, that is part of their attack on public schools.

A recent Gallup poll found that 90 percent of Americans ages 44 to 75 believed that the country is facing a retirement crisis. Nearly two-thirds were more fearful of depleting their assets than they were of dying. The fears about retirement are well placed — most Americans do not have enough retirement assets. It does not mean, however, that Social Security is in jeopardy. But if Republicans and Neo-liberals can scare enough people into believing that it is, then they can undercut Social Security.

Some would say that people should have been saving for their retirement. Perhaps, but how can they do so when while employed they often have no health insurance assistance, or when they tried to save and invest they were wiped out by the shenanigans of those abusing the financial sector? What if they avoided all that, only to discover that interest on savings is less than inflation, so that the mere act of saving puts them further behind?

Since when did republicans suddenly become such fiscal hawks? Since Barack Obama was elected President and the Republicans lost control of Congress, that's when. After frittering away a surplus, starting two wars on credit and giving the pharmaceutical industry the biggest government giveaway in history with no quibbling from anybody we now see what it is all about. The middle class and the poor will pay the bills racked up by the rich and powerful.

How are your dreams today?

Paying Attention: Now More Than Ever

As civil unrest around the world saturates our media, we need only focus on Madison, WI to see that we have pockets of resistance to unfair practices here at home. Oh, I know that even discussing unions is anathema to the socialist/communist fearing Texans and others of conservative persuasion. What a pity that we've needed unions everywhere to prevent our working men and women from continued exploitation, injury and death at the hands of negligent "businessmen."

If John L. Lewis hadn't organized the coal miners there is no telling how many deaths from unsafe mine explosions or the agony of long-term illness from black lung, never mind the pitiful wages that were just enough to keep the miners alive, but not enough for them to break out of their dependence on the "company store". How successful would the automakers of Detroit have been without those darned unions sucking profits off the top for (imagine this) a living wage whereupon a factory worker (horrors) could actually buy his own home, a car that he helped build and raise a family that wasn't clothed in rags?

This is NOT hyperbole. Those were the plights of those workers before unions saved them from total exploitation. In the mid-1970s teachers in Colorado Springs struck for the ability to form a collective bargaining unit. I happened to be working in the defense industry and was earning a whopping $13,000 per year. The teachers in Colorado Springs were making $7,500 – if they had more than 5 years on the job. Even in 1977 it was virtually impossible to raise a family on $7,500 before taxes. The results of gaining collective bargaining let teachers earn a living wage with yearly increases based on education and service to the district.

The union folks in Wisconsin simply don't want to lose their collective bargaining rights, rights they negotiated for and won. Now, the governor, in his race to fame wants to break the promises and the contracts in the spirit of fiscal responsibility. Thousands of union workers are in the streets demonstrating because they are being asked to pay for what the governor gave away to the wealthy and the corporations there. Tax breaks for the rich and the corporations, in case somebody missed it, is the Republican way to being fair. The people of Wisconsin are revolting against being exploited by the wealthy.

This is not unusual. Human beings have been exploiting other human beings for as long as recorded history. Here in the southern United States, the entire agrarian economy was predicated on that premise. We called it slavery. The nation had to fight its bloodiest and most horrific war over that issue. Today, and since the days of the great Ronald Reagan who went from union president to hypocrite, we call it union busting. Have you ever asked yourself why unions exist?

On April 20, 1914, the Rockefeller-owned coal mines, in the midst of a labor strike over terrible pay ($1.68 per day of "scrip" redeemable only at the company store) and very harsh working conditions, tried to break the strike by calling in the Colorado National Guard to force the workers back on the job. The ensuing riot killed 19 people including women and children. This became known as the Ludlow Massacre. This shocked the

Congress to finally pass legislation that outlawed scrip pay, resulted in the eight hour work day and child labor laws.

The anti-union actions over the last 30 years by conservative politics have reduced union representation from nearly 50% at the end of WW II to about 13% today. So, the canard about unions being the cause of our economic and budget woes is shallow and transparent; it is political posturing, nothing more.

If businesses and the management philosophy of public employees saw their employees as assets instead of liabilities, perhaps labor-management relations would be a lot more civil and a lot less confrontational. Perhaps the wage payers would see more productivity from employees that felt empowered and included instead of being treated like a necessary nuisance. This *enlightenment* would also allow that organized labor does NOT equal communism as the "sons" of Joe McCarthy understand it.

Americans want and deserve fairness and un-broken promises. Is that too much to ask of employers whether they be private or public? It appears that in Wisconsin, those employers don't care.

The Mad Rush to Fiscal Confusion

You read in several of my columns laments about low voter turnouts and subsequent events precipitated by those elected by a distinct minority of citizens. I recently watched an old George Carlin video from 1996 that offered a different perspective.

It's been said that if you don't vote, don't complain. Carlin says that he doesn't vote and that he will complain absolutely. He complains because those of us who voted put such inept, corrupt and stupid people in office and positions of power. He says we voters have no business complaining, because it is our fault that things got so screwed up. He has a point. My column last week complained about the shortage of capable people running for office and being elected; Carlin's snide comments start to make sense.

Our U.S. House of Representatives just passed a bill that temporarily kept the government from shutting down because the members of that body couldn't agree on a budget. In two more weeks, they'll do it again. This is from those we elected years ago and recently. Carlin has a right to complain.

The republicans in Congress want to cut about $60 billion from the public sector and social services agencies that try to do something good and positive for American citizens like educate them and treat their illnesses. A "conservative" estimate from the Management and Budget Office says that these cuts will cost over 700,000 jobs. Forgive my impertinence, but didn't these people run on the theme of "jobs, jobs, jobs"? We should complain, because we didn't get what we voted for.

The Texas legislature wants to cut social services like public education and Medicaid so they can balance the budget against an alleged $27 billion shortfall. At the same time the state Comptroller's office published a report that shows billions of uncollected tax dollars being exempted for one reason or another; about $22 billion from sales tax exemptions alone. Add to that a variety of energy related deductions and you see why we have such a huge budget problem. Does the republican dominated legislature want to do anything about these exemptions? Nope. They say that would amount to a tax increase and they vowed not to do that.

If you're having trouble following this, don't feel alone. The way I understand this is that we have taxes on the books that would, if allowed, cover our deficit *without* cutting any services. This begs the question: Who is benefitting from these tax exemptions? I don't know the answer to that, but I do know I'm not on that list. Carlin was right. It's our fault. We elected the "representatives" who think like this.

Rick Perry and Scott Walker in Wisconsin have much in common. They both want to deeply cut into funds that support public education. They both abhor teachers' unions. Of course, here in Texas, those unions are barely on the radar. Rick Perry refuses to accept $700,000 from the Federal government to educate our children. Scott Walker wants to destroy unions so he doesn't have to pay respectable wages. This happened after he gave away the state's surplus in tax cuts to corporations and the wealthy. Sound familiar? Perry doesn't want to be held accountable that the education money must go to education.

American citizens actually elected these "public servants" to look after us and our governments. We should all complain.

This sudden burst of budget hawking and fiscal "responsibility" is amazing in view of the great tax cuts that were supposed to create jobs, but didn't, the giveaway of a $200 billion surplus to the richest, borrowing trillions on a Chinese credit card to fight wars for no truthful reason and no end in sight. Why does nobody blink at spending $800 billion per year on defense and allow education and health to suffer as a result? Why do we spend $100 million on high stakes testing of our kids in Texas while their national test scores plummet?

Carlin is right. We are electing the wrong people to do the wrong things at the wrong time. We only have to look in the mirror to see who is responsible. At the same time, we will see who can fix the problem.

UPDATE: As of this writing, November, 2011, the budget and deficit issues still hang over the nation like the sword of Damocles. The republicans are refusing to do anything to generate more revenues while the Democrats are trying not to cut human services programs. A curious interim committee is being assigned the task to make a compromise by the end of this month. If they do not, certain mandatory cuts in defense spending will occur among other things.

This is the result of our election process. Somehow I can't imagine the good, thinking people of America sending people like these to represent them in Congress.

Taking Aim at Our Feet

This aphoristic title relates to inept hunters who, instead of bringing down game, end up shooting themselves in the foot. This has been applied to any number of people who screw up out of pure stupidity or remarkable ineptitude. This most recent spate of teacher bashing by the so-called budget hawks on the political right is confirming and redefining the meaning of this phrase.

There are many people out there who have not had good experiences in public schools during their childhood. Each is a special case with individual reasons. The tragic downside is that these unhappy souls look for ways to attack the education system in which they were not successful. The irony here is that they, as adults, will ensure that their children receive a poorer education than they did – if they get their way to cut salaries, jobs and general funding to public education.

The attack on the teachers in Wisconsin, now rippling outward like the waves from a pebble tossed into a fetid pond, is driving good, hard-working and dedicated people away from the profession. So, the whiners will see an even more serious deterioration of education quality via higher turnover, less qualified candidates and a host of other ills brought about by irresponsibly bashing the people who are caring for their children six to eight hours per day. Bang! One foot gone.

The other, more long-range issues involve the health and intellectual vigor of the country as a whole. Remember, all the great things that this country accomplished in its relatively brief history resulted from publicly educating children who grew up to do something great because they were prepared to do so. By completing the job that the Reagan administration failed to do (among its many failures), or even really attempted to do, destroying public education will push this country past the point of no return and guarantee its failure as a society. Bang! Both feet gone. All fall down.

One of the most important tasks I had as an industrial engineer and major capital project manager was to invest time and money in projects that were forward thinking and anticipated problems. When these "investments" were included in the project at the *beginning,* the project was almost always successful and returned the investment many times. What the budget hawks are trying to do to public education is about as short-sighted as anything I've ever seen in our history. If these cuts are made, the system is all but guaranteed to fail.

We have governors giving corporations tax breaks, promising to never raise any taxes for any reason, and promoting a scorched earth attack against labor, their unions if they exist and the people who are operating government at all levels. If the rush to smaller government becomes too intense, what is left will be the lowest of the low performers, the weakest of the weak leaders and the most incompetent of incompetent bureaucrats. This is a formula for societal collapse. If there was a third foot to blow off, these politicians would do that too.

Where was all this "fiscal responsibility" when a trillion dollar surplus was given to the rich in the form of a tax cut? Where were the budget hawks when we were lied to in order to go to war on a Chinese credit card? Where were the watchdogs of our banking systems when those banks went for the greed and nearly destroyed the economy of the western world? Oh. I remember. We had republicans ruling the Congress and in the White House.

We'll just never learn. Once again the republican machine to enrich the rich and attack the poorer classes is on the march. But this time they have gone too far. Instead of cutting fat, they are going after muscle and bone in their mad rush to feed the country to the rich on a platter made of the shattered dreams of working Americans who actually believed the promises of success through education and hard work. When somebody from the right screams, "This isn't class warfare", I have to laugh/cry. It most certainly IS class warfare. All you have to do is look at where the wealth has gone over the last 30 years to confirm that statement.

A World Without Oil

The next time you go shopping for anything, notice how everything is packaged. You'll find that almost everything you want from compost to bottled water to baby food is packaged in some form of plastic.

Plastic is everywhere. It is in our cars, our toys, our electronics devices, writing instruments, aka, pens and pencils, recording equipment, cameras, shopping bags, tool handles and wheelbarrows to name a few. Plastic is made from oil. Oil in the United States is about 80% imported. Fortunately, Canada and Mexico are two of our biggest suppliers for the oil we burn, but much more of it is sent to the countries from whom we buy so much of our merchandise, groceries and other consumables. They then send their products to us wrapped in plastic.

Last year, I wrote that it takes about an ounce of petroleum to produce a bottle of water with the same composition as most tap water and get it to the store. If you care to do the math, you'll find that the bottled water is almost 9 times as expensive as the gasoline that got you to the store. In that piece I also mentioned observations of people sitting in their idling vehicles for the sole purpose of staying cool, people solely driving enormous SUVs and dual-axle trucks to the store for groceries. As I scan our behaviors from the luxury of someone with too much time on his hands, one word keeps pinging in my brain: WASTE.

The petroleum resources that people are dying for are being wasted as much as they are being used up. What, for example, do we do with all the empty beverage containers, wrappers, razors, computers, cell phones and all the rest when we're done with them? We throw them in the trash and never give a second thought to their subsequent destination. Where all this processed oil ends up is in a dump, land fill (talk about misnomers) or burned somehow releasing more toxic chemicals into the air we breathe.

I am not a tree hugger, nor am I a squirrel feeder. I like to think of myself as a pragmatist who values what people live and die for. Every major oil-producing nation in the Middle East is in some sort of conflict that involves the killing of humans either directly or indirectly related to somebody's use of oil. That said I have to ask how those lives from battling over rapidly dwindling resources are valued. What good is this and the mayhem to come when the oil finally does run out? How do we justify our mountains of petroleum product waste in view of economic systems built on steady supplies of cheap oil?

Back in the day, beverages came in glass containers, some of which were re-cycled. Soup crackers were packed in wax paper instead of extruded plastic sleeves. Eggs were shipped in pressed paper cartons instead of Styrofoam. I carried my groceries and other purchases home in paper or canvas bags. My clothes were made with natural fibers. My athletic shoes were made from cowhide. My pencils were made of wood. My records were made of wax (Yes, I'm that old.). All our indoor and outdoor furniture were built from wood and metal.

I also do not deny the facts that many, many petroleum-based products have added immeasurable quality to everyone's life as well as to the medicines that keep us healthy from disease. My point is that we should want to extend those benefits for as long as possible until we can actually find ways to make affordable, non-petroleum replacements. Some day the oil will be gone-all of it. Guaranteed.

A good case for an alternative energy is biodiesel fuel replacing petro-diesel in some key areas. There are limits on the amount of biodiesel that can be made because of the amount of land (plants) or seashore (algae) required. Oils extracted from soybean, safflower and a variety of other oil-producing plants plus algal produced fuel make superb fuel for diesel engines. Diesel engines are designed to burn virtually anything flammable. Navy ships, jets, trucks, cars and generators all burn biodiesel more efficiently and with fewer polluting emissions than petro-diesel. It's cheaper to make than petro-diesel and ethanol and actually provides the same energy output as petro-diesel. So, naturally, the oil industry fostered a disinformation campaign while pressuring fuel outlets to quash the use of biodiesel. And so the story goes ....

Going Broke in Today's Atmosphere of Fear

"We're broke." So says E. J. Dionne's recent article in the Washington Post. He tells us that all our governments at every level are selling this line to justify draconian cuts in spending on social services and mindless attacks on the very small percentage of unionized state employees. The phrase is designed to create a sense of crisis that justifies rapid and radical actions before citizens have a chance to debate the consequences.

There is just one small problem: we're not broke. It is true that there is a fiscal problem based on tax cuts for the wealthy, an economic slump resulting from runaway greed, massive tax cuts for the rich, two wars on credit, a giveaway to drug companies and legalized theft by the banking and investment industries. But there is no crisis. There are many different ways to fix our problems in addition to just cutting by agenda-driven fiat. We have to realize that we are still a very rich country. Our unemployment rate remains at a stubborn 9%, or so. The stock market, though doing a lot of yo-yoing, is at or near 90% of record heights. The rich are doing exceptionally well.

Two of the loudest "We're broke!" advocates are John Boehner and Scott Walker, Governor of Wisconsin. "We're broke, broke going on bankrupt," Boehner said in a Feb. 28 Nashville speech. He's trying to justify the $61 billion spending cuts the House Republicans passed that will have negligible impact on the long-term deficit. Instead, future citizen investment programs like Head Start, student loans and a variety of other pro-person items are the targets of this Chicken Little nonsense.

Walker used the "we're broke" canard to justify his attack on public-worker collective bargaining rights. Yet the state's supposedly "broke" status came after he approved tax cuts to the rich and the corporations in Wisconsin. This is the worst kind of cynicism, especially when Walker told a Koch brother impersonator that "this is our time to change the course of history." The only history I see being changed is the replacement of democracy by a plutocracy of his rich pals.

In both cases, the fiscal issues are just an excuse for ideologically driven policies to lower taxes on well-off people and businesses while reducing government programs that the Republican brand has been attacking for almost 80 years. They just don't seem to understand that this is a nation of people, not money.

Boehner's statement is, of course, simply wrong. As Bloomberg's David J. Lynch wrote: "The U.S. today is able to borrow at historically low interest rates, paying 0.68 percent on a two-year note that it had to offer at 5.1 percent before the financial crisis began in 2007. Financial products that pay off if Uncle Sam defaults aren't attracting unusual investor demand. And tax revenue as a percentage of the economy is at a 60-year low, meaning if the government needs to raise cash and can summon the political will, it could do so."

As one might expect, the republican politics use a phony metaphor to hijack the nation's political conversation and skew public policies to benefit better-off Americans and hurt most others. This is not news. Republicans have been representing this big lie for decades.

Dionne continues: "We have an 8.9 percent unemployment rate, yet further measures to spur job creation are off the table. We're broke, you see. We have a $15 trillion economy, yet we pretend to be an impoverished nation with no room for public investments in our future or efforts to ease the pain of a deep recession on those Americans who didn't profit from it or cause it in the first place." Remember back to the last election cycle when Republicans campaigned on "jobs, jobs, jobs"?

Sen. Al Franken (D-Minn.) pointed out in a little-noticed speech on the economy in December, "...during the past 20 years, 56 percent of all income growth went to the top 1 percent of households. Even more unbelievably, a third of all income growth went to just the top one-tenth of 1 percent." So how does anyone justify cutting taxes for the wealthy? Obviously cutting their taxes DID NOT create any jobs.

Franken noted that "...when you adjust for inflation, the median household income actually declined over the last decade." So, we see that those folks *are* going broke, yet because the Republicans tell us "we're broke," we can't possibly help those who need it most. How else do you define class warfare?

Making Points That Matter

The other day I was promoting an excellent charity benefitting kids and ended up having a great conversation with one of its patrons. The subject turned to politics and the difficulties in our society. We talked about how President Obama blew his (and our) chance to fix the broken country left him (and us) from the previous eight years of mismanagement and greed. We lamented the lack of leadership and courage that should have steamrolled the republican "NO" machine and gotten more important things done than indeed did get done. This is a tough call because the Obama administration has accomplished many, many things in the last two years; some of which I've mentioned in this column.

The conversation drifted to what a good, solid democrat should do to get the attention of the people away from the straight politics-by-fear strategy of the Rove-influenced republicans and the mindlessness of the Tea Party. We agreed that a list of bullet points presented clearly and firmly would remind many independents of why they voted democrat for so many years, and why they should vote that way again. Here is my list of "bullet" points that some intrepid democrat might use some day....soon.

- Dump the public education gimmicks like NCLB and Race to the Top. Replace them with responsible, classroom teacher oriented actions that do not emphasize punishment. Proactive teacher development and professional salary structures must be included as well as a longer school year.
- Remove the $106,000 cap on Social Security contributions. Reduce SSA benefits for those collecting over $50,000 annually from other sources on a sliding scale.
- Install pay-as-you-go budget expenditures in the House. If the money isn't there, the project doesn't get done. Raise taxes on the wealthiest to pre-Bush II levels. The tax "cuts" didn't create jobs, so we may as well balance the budget instead.
- Overturn the Glass-Steagall repeal so that banks won't be tempted to do what they just did and almost destroyed the world's economy.
- Overturn the *Citizens United* decision by the U.S. Supreme Court that allows corporations to commit unlimited, anonymous funds to political candidates. The repeal of this naked, cynical and craven misinterpretation of the First Amendment will return the election process to the citizens of the country.
- Re-install *Workfare* wherein chronically unemployed people are trained to do productive work. Two years is adequate time for someone to be trained and put to work or risk losing their government assistance.
- Institute universal, single-payer health care for every man, woman and child of American citizenship by expanding Medicare's system. Payroll taxes by both employee and employer will provide the funding; large scale negotiation leverage will keep costs under control and prevent windfall profits through exploitation of the sick. A key addition here is strengthening the fraud investigation and prosecution of criminal activity.
- Close all tax-avoidance loopholes for hiding money in foreign banks.

53

- End tax incentives for sending jobs overseas; replace them with incentives to create new ones in the United States.
- End filibuster rules in the U.S. Senate. Make lobbying illegal.
- End all oil company subsidies. Offer tax incentives for investing in and successfully developing alternative energy sources and uses primarily involving renewable energy.
- Re-hire the laid-off OSHA, EPA and FDA inspectors and increase their authority to shut down safety, environmental and health violators. Add inspectors to imported goods at points of entry.
- End the wars in Afghanistan and Iraq. Cut $200 billion from the Pentagon budget for investment into alternative energy research and development with the 5-year goal of becoming independent of middle-eastern oil imports.

This list of talking points is, in my opinion, the beginning of the long road back to greatness that corrupt politicians, corporate oligarchies and greedy financiers have kept us from taking. In order to begin making these points reality another great shift in attitude and energy from the American people is required. We can no longer expect greatness and "exceptionalness" without stepping up and voting. A 48% turnout of registered voters for national, general elections is how dictators and plutocratic governments come to power.

I'm betting that the American people are rapidly waking up to the fact that splinter organizations like the Tea Party are destroying the things that made us great.

Hypocrisy Unlimited

It's hard to address this topic because there are so many places to begin. I'll just start with my favorite intellectual dwarf, Newt Gingrich, a presidential wannabe. His commentary about President Obama's decision making process for the Libyan adventure flipped directions 3 different times over two weeks. I guess he thinks everyone's memory is as short as his.

The elephant of hypocrisy in the room is labeled "JOBS"! The Republicans found ways to campaign on that theme enough to fool voters into thinking that they would fulfill their campaign promises. The great budget cuts proposed by the House Republicans will also cause between 700,000- 1 million jobs to be lost. That which passes for government in Austin, Texas also wields sharp pencils in order to squeeze deficit blood from the no-tax turnip. The bad news is that nearly 400,000 Texas jobs will be lost as a result. This scenario is being repeated in states across the nation where Republicans control their congress.

The hypocrisy here is manifold. First, as in Wisconsin, corporations and the wealthy enjoy the best of tax breaks and exemptions, thus reducing revenue generation for government. Then the republicans pledge "no more taxes" as a way to further enable the already enabled greed present in us all. Finally, the "starving the beast" philosophy causes jobs to be lost and economic growth to come to a screeching halt. Just ask the Britons, the Portuguese and the Greeks how well that is working for them.

Paul Krugman's article in the 3/25/2011 New York Times reminds us all that the overwhelming majority of economists who actually know what they are doing have said all along that cutting spending before creating jobs is absolutely the WRONG approach to economic recovery. So, naturally, our legislators do just the opposite. In our case, the Republican dominated House's hypocrisy morphs into abject stupidity and the so-called conservative state legislatures follow blindly along.

For over 100 years economists have said and proven that jobs and work are the best and surest tonics for maintaining a healthy economy. It doesn't hurt that everyone pays their fair share of taxes either. This pill is truly bitter especially when you hear Republicans telling us how favorable they are to the working man then help their corporate pals send the jobs overseas so that unions won't form and then tax those who DO retain employment to pay for the tax breaks for the wealthy and the corporations.

This is hypocrisy gone haywire. It is government by those who choose not to govern, but rather exploit loopholes and weaknesses in the most vulnerable classes of people of the nation. How can these politicians tell us out of one side of their mouths how precious our children are, then turn around and cut their education funding, trump up yet another idiotic bureaucracy (Race to the Top) and pretend that the teachers are at fault if the kids fail? How can they tell us how much they respect those seniors who gave their working lives to better the nation and the lives of others, then turn around and cut the supporting programs those revered elders have depended on for a dignified retirement?

Hypocrisy Unlimited – Part II

A friend, true American and patriot sent me this little homily: "It takes time to create a masterpiece! The people who began the creation of our American masterpiece also created our Declaration of Independence, they fought and won that independence, they created our Constitution and its Bill of Rights. We continue to provide the best of each generation to defend this masterpiece against those who wish to destroy it. There are now 197 million white people, 38 million black people, 51 million Hispanics, 15 million Asians and 9 million "other" people from various ethnic and racial/interracial groups in the United States. In another 25-30 years the white majority will be replaced with the results of the true *melting pot,* and the masterpiece will be complete!" The author of this somewhat edited comment is a 76 year old Texan who served in the Air Force and is currently being kept alive by the Veterans Administration.

I mention this to show that not all things governmental are bad and evil.

Someone also sent me a list of all the state agencies, offices and departments from the state of California and asked the idiotic question: "Do you wonder why California is broke"? The obvious response to this kind of ridiculous and shallow questioning is that California wouldn't exist as a civilized entity in 2011 without most of them, especially the education agencies. As late as the 1970s California had the finest public and higher education systems in the country. I attended San Diego State University from 1971-1974 and earned a Master of Science degree for the grand total of $785 for tuition and books. Then came the tax whiners during Reagan's reign as governor. The resulting "Prop. 13" property tax cut slammed the schools and university systems to the point where they are now barely mediocre. I find it more than a little ironic that Republican governors who become President tend to destroy the things that made our country something to envy by the rest of the world. Our children and their education pay the price for their political hubris.

Another friend recently lamented how she felt the "conservative" wing of the Republican Party has hijacked Christianity and turned their version of it into a political weapon. She went on to say that the preoccupation with abortion and women's rights was simply hypocritical especially since those who claimed to be pro-life led with their "faith" on the one hand, but denied those children born to poor, unwed, teenage mothers help from public charity...just as Jesus would have done. She said she had recently re-read the books of Matthew and Luke and had her faith in the generosity of one person to the next renewed and justified. She wondered why so many "conservatives" couldn't see their hypocrisy on this issue.

We decided that it was perhaps a cynical political ploy to attract more people to a particular voting bloc than it was to execute the Biblical passages pertaining to *Christian Charity.* Perhaps the masterpiece isn't quite finished after all.

The current NCAA basketball tournament is raging on. Most of the players in the tournament will not graduate from college even after exhausting their 4 years of scholarship eligibility. This is also true in most major men's college athletic programs. There are a few stellar exceptions like the Notre Dame football program, but most "student athletes" are in college athletics to either take a shot at the pros or just escape their lives in poorer surroundings. I am sympathetic to the kids who are recruited out of the ghettos of America to play college sports. For most of them this will be their only opportunity to see life outside the environment of drugs and thugs. Good for them. I wish them nothing but good fortune whether they graduate or not.

But isn't it hypocritical for major academic institutions to label these youngsters "*student* athletes" when so few earn degrees? I recently learned that the term *student athlete* was coined by the NCAA to avoid being sued for labor law violations. Isn't it hypocritical of the NCAA to allow the universities to reap huge revenues from their athletic programs while penalizing the kids for having someone buy them a dinner? Ask Tiger Woods why he turned pro before graduating from Stanford and you'll know the answer.

The "masterpiece" is not yet complete after all.

The 400

A recent *Newsweek* article stated that there are 400 individuals in this country who own more wealth than just over 50% of the other Americans. As astounding as that statistic is, equally disturbing is the fact that 90% of wage earners have received a whopping $280 per year raise in actual earnings over the last 30 years while the top 1%er's share of the national income has doubled from 9% in 1977 to 20% today. The richest 0.1% of that top 1%'s share has tripled. That means that only 150,000 households (the top 0.1%) now "earn" as much as the bottom 120 *million* households combined.

So, how do you feel about the richest retaining their tax cuts now? G.E., the largest corporation in American hasn't paid any taxes at all for the last few years. So, how are you and your tax lawyer doing about hiding your income in the Cayman Islands? I'm guessing the next time somebody whines about our government trying to "redistribute the wealth", you might ask them where they fit into this arrangement. Ask them how they're paying for their child's higher education. Ask them what they think their fair share of the American money machine is.

The fact is that our inequality of wealth rivals that of the worst *banana republics* we used to despise. WE are the banana republic now, at least with regard to wealth distribution and the vast differences between how poor people try to live while the richest keep buying jets, yachts and multi-million dollar homes for part-time residence on lakes. Do you suppose some of those poor people might like to see a little largesse thrown their way in the form of a job that pays enough to allow thoughts about raising a family or sending a kid to college?

Parents can send their children to school, but they can't force them to learn. Learning has to be voluntary. That volunteerism has to come from motivation. The motivation has to come from a vision of a future for which that learning will prepare them. In this sense, history is the greatest teacher known to humans, because we are the only organism that can process very long term history, history that preceded our lifetimes. Long-term history teaches us, presumably, to avoid making the same mistakes as our ancestors. That is how we managed to get to 2011 as the most dominant species on Earth over the last 50,000 years.

The point here is that we in America don't seem to have learned the history lessons of medieval economies and societies. Even ancient Egypt, whose artifacts fill museums around the world, doesn't seem to faze us as we allow the ruling class to become smaller and richer while the general population becomes bigger and poorer – and not for want of resources. Ancient Rome, which overlapped Egypt's last dynasties, rotted from within when an oligarchy usurped power from their grand experiment in representative government and handed it to one man.

What amazes me is the number of people actually promoting this shift toward an oligarchy that will take food out of their own mouths, roofs from over their head and education away from their children. Those oligarch wannabes will NOT qualify for the 400

Club, yet they carry on as if they will be part of the show instead of just the stagehands sweating way behind the scenes.

Will it take that final drama when the 400 finally slam the door on the rest of us, suspend the Constitution and usurp all law and finance from the 300 million before people wake up to the fact that they've given the country away to the few while all the while whining about some interpretation of the word *socialism* which is clearly not understood? Those who currently dismiss Michael Moore's documentaries out of hand will hate to remember the scene from *Capitalism: A Love Story* where the banks sent letters describing their intent for a plutocratic takeover of all finance in the United States and a good portion of the Western world. The 400 will make it so.

Unscrambling the Code

It begins with news of the day. Today is 8 April 2011. Our Congress in Washington cannot reach a budget agreement to allow the government to function. Why? The Tea Party caucus wants to defund Planned Parenthood, that's why. I hasten to point out that the Tea Party created itself on the basis of fiscal responsibility. Clearly that is not the case. *Fiscal responsibility* becomes code for not providing any care for at-risk women while also usurping a woman's control over her own life and body-oriented decisions.

The Tea Party says they want to adhere to the Constitution as written by the founding fathers. Great. That is code for we don't want people of color to vote or own property; women needn't bother to vote either. It is code for eliminating the Bill of Rights, because they were not part of the original manuscript. It is also code for a particular xenophobia that fears and resents anybody who isn't exactly like them. I say this from direct experience with one of their blogs.

Your intrepid columnist participated in a Tea Party blog that had a disclaimer disallowing any commentary that wasn't strictly down company lines. Almost immediately following the disclaimer was a trumpeting of the glory of the Constitution and the First Amendment. I was immediately on-guard. Then I started reading comments from bloggers.

Do you remember that pang of fear we used to get when we saw something really, really wrong happening? I experienced that pang when I read the wildly extreme commentary that was filled with code words (members were not allowed to write racist comments) and disrespectful terms for our President and how he is what is wrong with EVERYTHING in America and only his ouster will bring all of us back to the fold, etc., etc. Then there was this guy who threatened to throw all non-believers out of airplanes if they didn't think and believe like him. I'm not making this up.

The code to decipher here is that of extremism and what it says. Having just completed William Shirer's *The Nightmare Years: 1930-1940,* I admit I was a little sensitized to National Socialist rhetoric. What I read on this Tea Party blog scared me to my bones that such a nationally recognized political organization could actually exist today. The hatefulness heaped on another group (fill in your own code words), the virulent hatred directed at anyone not as far right as they (think of Hitler's blind hatred of Socialism), and the distorted history and facts used to justify an agenda advocating the replacement of our current government were especially disturbing. You didn't need a code book to see where this was going. Today it was about politics and spending and taxes. But those were code words for something seemingly much more sinister.

I have also had conversations with other, more level-headed Tea Party members and did not see or hear this level of extremism. These individuals do feel put upon by an unfair tax system (who doesn't), but who created it? These folks think that we spend too much on social programs. It's true. We do. What isn't answered is which ones are overfunded and by how much. Sane Tea Party members talk about smaller government, but can't define what size it should be and where it should be trimmed.

The code book says that all this splintering and confusion amongst the various wings of the Tea Party is because the people who call themselves members of this group don't really know what they want. They don't know if all their complaints about spending should be directed at Obama or not. Since the President is not in charge of the budget, that seems pointless at best. So why blame him for everything? The decoded answer, I think, is that they don't know what to do with this kind of President ...in whatever code one wants to use.

Obama doesn't write the budget, Congress does. Who elects the Congress? We do. Since so few of us actually vote, I'd say we have nobody to blame but ourselves. Voting is code for: Taking charge and responsibility for the country, the Constitution and the laws. If you don't vote, don't complain.

The Alchemy of Conservatism

For all the right reasons, modern science, employing empirical methods, superseded alchemy. Alchemy was based on the "received wisdom" or "common knowledge" found in ancient texts saying all things were made of the four "prime elements": earth, air, fire and water. The Renaissance (14th -17th Centuries) was a transition time between alchemy acceptance as legitimate knowledge about the world and the time when it was rejected and replaced by the empirical scientific method - the science that is practiced in every modern university today.

America has been in the midst of a similar transition since the 1980s until today, only in reverse! Before the 1980s, American politics was dominated by practical humanistic values. The Supreme Court looked at the social mores of the day and rejected the theory of "separate but equal" in our schools, (irrespective of those clinging to past prejudices) and desegregated them. Earlier, FDR's administration rejected the "balance the budget to stimulate employment" mantra that was the "received wisdom" of the country and embraced Keynesian economics because there was empirical evidence that it worked!

With the 1980s and the ascendency of what we call conservatism, all empirical economic evidence was rejected out of hand. An entire propaganda machine was created with the single purpose of turning the clock back to a time when myths trumped empiricism...when alchemy trumped science. The Heritage Foundation, Cato Institute, right wing talk radio, Glenn Beck and the rest of the "conservative" *intelligencia*, devoted themselves to create a grand rewrite of our history and inserted a mythology, implemented by Grover Norquist, with Ronald Reagan as the front man.

That mythology was created and promulgated throughout the country...indeed, the world! This mythology embraced the following false elements: Reagan lowered taxes...balanced the budget...created millions of new jobs...never negotiated with terrorists...won the Cold War single-handedly...proved that debt does not matter...established that the government is always inept and that publicly supported education, at any level, is to be rejected in favor of the GOP mythical partly line of private enterprise for everything. In short, Reagan rescued America from the corrupting influence of liberalism, internationalism and collectivism and made us a "shining city on a hill."

So well did Norquist do his job that millions of people still buy into the great Reagan myth. It is axiomatic, in most "conservative" circles, that cutting taxes creates jobs or balances a budget, though no one can explain how or show that it ever has! Supposedly compassionate, conservative voters are demanding that their elected representatives take food out of the mouths of hungry children, deny women disease prevention opportunities and cut seniors retirement funds in order to reduce the national debt. The same people still think that every government program and agency is corrupt, incompetent, and prevents businessmen from making a profit. Anyone who thinks otherwise is labeled a *socialist* with strong negative connotations.

Today, the conservative "economic wisdom" says we must compare our tax code with the dysfunctional tax codes of the rest of the world - those who have bought into the Reagan myth abroad - instead of the history of our own tax code in post WWII period here in the United States. What worked in this country prior to 1980 must be, by the conservative myth, rejected as tainted by liberal revisionist history. *Keynesian economic principles could not have rescued us from the Great Depression, not because there is no evidence that it did, but because empirical evidence cannot – as a matter of faith – be allowed to contradict the conservative alchemy.*

Americans born after 1965 were inculcated with this "conservative" mythological dogma, a mythology where none of the claims are true! There is not a shred of empirical evidence to suggest that anything that the myth of *Supply-side economics* says happened in the Reagan administration actually *did* happen. Should anyone wonder, therefore, that we have "birther" members of the Tea Party setting the agenda for the Republican Party? Should we be surprised that vast numbers of people are willing to vote against their own economic interest and savage our social safety nets by believing in the Reagan myth?

The political wisdom of conservative America is built upon a body of false information! The conservatives have abandoned reason and empirical evidence and chased after a vision of an America that never was and never will be. The alchemists have returned and are doing their best to create a failed state.

Manufacturing America: Now More Than Ever

Since the end of World War II, the trend in American manufacturing has been to offload work to cheaper labor markets. From 1946 until about 2000, just about every other country was a cheaper labor market than the USA's. As countries like Japan and Germany regained their industrial vigor with our help, they used our technology to innovate manufacturing processes to produce very high quality, reliable products in all consumer product areas. Now, those countries and many others dominate the consumption monkey in our society.

What have we been doing....?
- Since 2001 we have closed 42,000 factories.
- Dell announced it is closing its last large manufacturing plant in the U.S. eliminating 900 jobs.
- We manufacture zero (0) cell phones.
- Since 2000, 5.5 million manufacturing jobs have vanished, about 32%.
- Between 1998-2008 the employment gain of U.S. affiliates overseas operations increased by 10.1 million while declining by 21 million here.
- In 1959, manufacturing was 28% of our GNP. In 2008 it was 11.5%.
- In 2009, less than 12 million Americans worked in manufacturing, nearly the same as 1941. Then our population was about135 million, today it's over 310 million.
- 70% of today's GDP comes from consumption.
- Today nearly 50 million Americans live in poverty, the highest number since records began 51 years ago and the highest, per capita, among "first world" nations. (Source: Frosty Troy, editor, The Oklahoma Observer, Vol. 43, No. 7)

This data illustrates how eager American businesses are to avoid paying American workers living wages. The recent geological events in Japan have, ironically, shown how truly fragile this global economy can be when Mother Nature states her case.

The GM plant in Shreveport, LA builds Chevrolet trucks. One of the 20,000 parts is made in Japan near where the devastation occurred. It is cheaper for GM to buy the part from Japan rather than make it here, but without that part, the assembly line stops and 923 workers are furloughed.

Ford also imports paint pigments from Japan for its black and red automobiles. No pigments, no paint, and no black or red cars come out the end of the factories; workers get laid off.

Toyota *Tundra* trucks are built in San Antonio, TX. The rear axles are made by Hino Motors in Arkansas. Hino imports a critical gear from its factory in Japan. With *just-in-time* deliveries in force, the Arkansas inventory is depleted per the production schedule predicated on regular receipt of parts from Japan. The gear plant in Japan was destroyed by the tsunami. The ripple effect is that 2,800 Texas workers will be laid off for lack of these parts in Arkansas. Hino workers there will be affected also.

Add to these stories the fact that 84% of our printed circuit boards are made overseas and there is a security issue involved. All of our military and surveillance electronic equipment use printed circuit boards as the basis for their operational hardware. The boards cost less from overseas, but they are not made here. The number of those boards made overseas used in our critical and security systems is not known to this author (Source: Jim Hightower, The Oklahoma Observer, Vol.43, No.7).

The point here is that in the mad rush to maximize profit we may have passed a threshold for securing our own nation. We've known for decades how poorly American corporate management regards its labor force, but that bias should not and cannot be used to weaken our country and destroy the middle class.

The main things we build are automobiles, airplanes and military hardware. Cleverly, the military-industrial complex has created an archipelago of sites in every state and in the largest districts so that politicians are loath to cut wasteful operations or close bases in their districts to avoid political suicide.

So, as Stan said to Ollie: "This is another fine mess you've gotten us into." As someone recently wrote to me, "...maybe we don't need to educate anybody, because we don't build anything anyway." There is this other archipelago of connected islands between good-paying jobs, money and consumption. If our people have poor-paying or no jobs, how are they going to consume? If our corporate moguls don't want us to manufacture anything, what will we build? I guess we'll just leave it to the gods of *free market enterprise* like we did in the 1920s. That didn't work out so well, did it?

How Does Your Garden Grow?

Even with the extreme drought, my water well is still doing *well*. My garden is watered by automatic timers connected to a home-made drip line that uses water conservatively, yet provides sufficient moisture for growing my vegetables. As of this writing, the tomatoes are almost 2 feet tall and producing green fruit. The onions will be finished in another month as will the potatoes and salad greens. All the other producing plants are growing beautifully and look to produce what we need for the summer and fall.

My garden is not strictly organic, but I do use goat manure composted from my in-law's barn to provide the nitrogen and organic material for good, healthy vegetables. The growing/harvesting season where I live lasts from January to November. Early crops will be replaced with black-eyed peas and okra and I'll pick them until first frost. I like to think I get maximum productivity out of my 1,200 square feet of growing space. I'll let you know how good the cantaloupe is this year.

The point here is that if water and fertilizer are withheld, my plants will not grow, or if they do, poorly. This fact also applies to a capitalistic economy. Without capital, businesses cannot grow or even come into being. Without new businesses and growing older ones, jobs aren't created. When jobs aren't created there is no money for workers to buy things that stimulate more production and market growth.

What my father-in-law's goats do in the barn is the same thing as what taxes and other revenues do to capitalism: they produce (cash) and compost (interest) the fertilizer so that it can be used to grow other things. I say again: without this neat ecological loop, growth will be minimal at best. So why are banks and corporations sitting on all that "cash" instead of spreading it out to grow the garden of jobs and prosperity? I see jobs as the bee brush the goats eat to produce the organic "capital" in the barn.

Corporate America, however, is sending our cash to other barns than our own. At the same time, the banks and corporate America are sending our jobs to other countries because of perceived cheaper labor and because it makes the quarterly profit reports look good. Here is a summary from Senator Bernie Sanders showing how some of our largest corporations and banks are re-paying the American public for allowing them to exist.

- **Exxon-Mobil:** 2009 profits of $19 billion; $156 million IRS rebate; NO Federal taxes.
- **Bank of America:** 2010 profit of $4.4 billion; $1 trillion bailout; $1.9 billion IRS refund.
- **G. E.:** 5-year profit $26 billion; $4.1 billion IRS refund; 20% of U.S. jobs sent elsewhere; $0 U.S. taxes paid.
- **Chevron:** 2009 profits $10 billion; $19 million IRS refund.
- **Valero Energy:** $68 billion in sales; $157 million IRS refund; 3-year tax break of $134 million.
- **Goldman-Sachs:** 2008 profit $2.3 billion; Paid 1.1% of their taxes; $800 billion bailout.
- **Citigroup:** 2010 profit $4 billion; $0 U.S. taxes paid; $2.5 trillion bailout.

- **Conoco-Phillips:** 2007-2009 profit $16 billion; $451 million in tax breaks.

Last year I summarized how the rich hide their taxable income in foreign banks to the tune of $140 billion in uncollected tax revenue. These are the same people screaming for more tax relief. Don't you feel good about that? By the way, we are the only industrialized country that taxes earnings made in foreign countries and returned home. So, in defense of our corporate accountants, they absolutely lack incentive to bring the capital to the United States for investment in OUR people's job opportunities. Meantime, these "foreign" assets help companies' stocks look good while that makes more money for those who own that stock.

These numbers boggle the mind as to the potential of available capital that could prime the job creation pump. So why are these industries and banks sitting on all this capital while they exploit our wildly unfair tax code to avoid investing in the country that allows them to exist? Why are they denying our economy and our workers the opportunity to be great?

It seems to this intrepid writer that the moral fiber of corporate America has fallen on hard ground and is denying that ground the nutrients it needs to grow jobs and hopes and dreams of the people who depend on it to do so. What is the intent of this dismantling of successful commerce, to deny the American worker everything he/she hoped for in the name of profit? Or are there other, more sinister intents...like creating a ruling plutocracy of the few.

Complaints Deserve Solutions

How many times have we each been caught complaining and/or whining about something our government or some other "authority" does that we don't like? Inevitably, somebody says, "Well, what would you do, wise guy?" It happens to me a lot, because I complain a lot. Here I go off into my world of solutions to complaints I and others have made and what I see as plausible solutions.

THE BUDGET: Raise the debt ceiling so the world economy doesn't collapse while we continue to embarrass ourselves on the world economic stage. Because we are the largest player in international economics, when we screw up and get greedy, everybody follows, hence the world's recession. The first thing to do is cut spending where there is overkill (defense) or "traditional" waste (oil company subsidies). Next, close all loopholes to tax avoidance especially for offshore bank accounts and overseas profits for American based corporations. Move the top tax bracket to 40% and give tax incentives to those who create jobs. Take the cap off Social Security contributions. This dovetails with alternative energy investment and development.

ENERGY: Take the money cut from defense and sponsor research and project funding for alternate energy until feasible and economically viable technologies can replace foreign oil imports from Asia and the Middle East. I see this as a win-win situation in that we will actually become energy independent from those countries who hate us, our religion and our form of government. Since we won't have to fight these people over control of the oil, it will justify the reduction in defense spending. This action will dovetail into developing a new, more consistent and intelligent foreign policy.

FOREIGN POLICY: We need to share our technological breakthroughs with the rest of the world and form economic alliances to keep everybody's cost of implementation down while weaning everyone away from Middle East oil. If we do this intelligently, the religious-based schisms between the West and the Middle East will be greatly defused and the cash will be closer to everyone's home. We should also continue to share our food and medical technology with the poorest nations and encourage our economic partners to do the same. Inclusive of this is an education system teaching people how to control their populations so that more of them can be well-fed and healthy. It wouldn't hurt if we did that here for our population segments that over-reproduce for the available ability to feed the children adequately.

EDUCATION: Scrap *No Child Left Behind* and *Race to the Top*. Neither of these programs is worth the money they consume for the results they get. Spend the money on recruiting and developing teachers and administrators that concern themselves with educating children rather than passing tests. This is a long-term issue and results from excellence in teaching will take 2 or 3 cohorts getting all the way through to show the impact on society. Pay for teacher education. Pay teacher salaries equivalent to their equally educated peers in business and industry. Develop a national curriculum that will prepare both academically AND vocationally oriented students to meet business's needs for the rest of the century. Lengthen the school year while making sure teachers develop lessons that incorporate real-life examples.

POVERTY: We've known for decades that poor kids do less well in school and in life than wealthier kids. Fifteen percent of our population is chronically destitute; it may be more. They reside, primarily, in our inner-cities. I propose a massive series of urban renewal projects conducted by those very citizens who live in run-down neighborhoods. Train them and give them the materials and the financial incentive to work their way out of poverty as well as make the cities livable. This dovetails with the advances in education proposed above.

My vision sees the need for greater participation of our citizenry to stave off societal collapse from the greedy few taking our wealth and our resources to other countries and leaving us with nothing. We must give all our citizens a reason to work toward excellence in everything they do not just for the money they can make, but for the security they gain for their families and our way of life. It doesn't get more patriotic than that.

How Theories Become Laws

One of my favorite readers commented on my last column about myths and theories as they pertain to economics in America. He argued that we should be more attuned to what a theory is versus a myth. Okay. As a scientist, I agree with that.

A theory is an idea stemming from facts and circumstances. In order to prove or disprove the theory, one must conduct experiments or tests using the correct factors pertaining to the elements (variables) of the theory. You can't test a theory about pitching to left-handed batters, for example, if you're using croquet balls instead of baseballs.

To have a theory become law all the results from all the tests must be the same to a very high degree of statistical confidence. The length and complexity of the tests are a function of the number and type of variables that must be part of each experiment. Changing some variables and conducting tests to those changes help prove or disprove a theory. If the variables are many, testing may take a very long time. If some of the outcomes show promise in validating the theory, it is incumbent on the testing regime to drive toward statistical validation. If the outcomes tend to show invalidation, then perhaps the theory should be replaced by another that shows more positive results to the intent of that theory.

One economic theory that has been tried several times continues to confound testing and economists as to its validity. That would be *Supply Side Economic Theory.* This is the brainchild of Milton Friedman who was awarded the Nobel Prize in Economics for introducing this theory to other less worthy souls.

Some of my conservative friends think that the Nobel Prize is often awarded prematurely to those in a popular cause or position. I agree. Barack Obama was awarded the Nobel Peace Prize for not being George Bush. Similarly, Milton Friedman was awarded his Nobel for a theory that has yet to yield validating data. Both of these awards preceded anticipated results from the awards committee.

Prior to the *Progressive Movement* of the 1920s and 30s, our economic theories looked a lot like the scenario Friedman set up in his theory. There were totally unregulated businesses exploiting a very poor and ignorant working class that had no financial hope of escaping their lot. Child labor laws did not exist, so families with children had to send their sons and daughters into unventilated factories and mines for a dollar a day in order to feed themselves. There were the big, financial and industrial moguls who hoarded capital and wealth because they could. Sound familiar? There were no anti-trust laws and price-fixing was normal to business. There was NO health care of any type for anyone except the moguls or super rich of the day. There was no unemployment insurance. There were no retirement plans. There was no income tax. In fact there were very few ways that our government could raise revenue to pay for its military or fund research and innovative projects.

These conditions, in other, less "sophisticated" countries without a Constitution defining Democracy, resulted in armed and violent rebellion by the have-nots against the government often overthrowing it and wresting economic control from the moguls. I guess the largesse of the rich didn't quite trickle down far or fast enough for the starving masses.

In the United States, we reformed our laws and amended our Constitution to avoid armed rebellion and revolution. The horrors of labor/management warfare and the growing influence of unions forced our government to change the laws and facilitate more equity between the wealthy and working classes. These actions from the *Progressive Era* gave us the middle class who became the consumer class that grew businesses big and small. It wasn't supply side economics that allowed this quiet revolution. It was intelligent government that cared about ALL of its people, not just the rich, that avoided social catastrophe.

The main reason this was accomplished was because the *living* Constitution allowed our government to do it. Strict adherence to the letter of the Constitution is like a religious fundamentalist who cannot see the marvelous opportunities for flexibility and benefit by allowing intellect into the experiment.

Theories and Laws – Part II

This part of the thought process concerning laws evolving from theories, takes me back to an interview I saw with the Nobel laureate, Milton Friedman many years after his work on supply side economic theory. When the interviewer, a son of a major pharmaceutical family, asked Friedman about the concept of raising taxes to pay off debt, Friedman dismissed the question by saying that taxes were socialist and should be very limited. When asked how taxes should be used as a function of a country's operation, Friedman threw up his hands, called the interviewer a socialist and ended the interview.

Friedman's work was latched onto by the Republican Party and turned into a political position by the unknown Grover Norquist. Norquist is an ultra-conservative think tank type who found glory, but not much notoriety by schooling front man Ronald Reagan in the wonders of "trickle down" theory such that it got him elected twice and the intents of Friedman's theory brought into practice.

The prior Carter administration experienced extreme financial hostility from banking America who were and are pulling major strings in the Federal Reserve and Department of Treasury. His administration was doomed by high inflation and astronomical interest rates that stalled any economic and personal growth. Then, we got Reagan and his cabal of supply-siders.

After cutting taxes in half for the rich and a little for the "lower" classes, away we went on the great experiment in trickle down. Well, the only things that trickled were profits and financial gain *upward* for the richest Americans. The working and middle classes saw their earnings and spending power stagnate – at best. Then came the military buildup and Reagan found himself in a fiscal nutcracker that required that he raise taxes; something his administration had to do 11 times to come close to balanced budget – a major component of Supply Side economic theory.

After 8 years of this experiment, the country was left holding a $6 trillion bag of debt that Ronnie's successor, Mr. *Voodoo Economics*, George H.W. Bush had to deal with. Bush got himself elected by promising "no new taxes", then found himself adding new taxes to pay off the debt and balance the budget.

At this point, one would expect that some very smart economists would have seen that cutting taxes while spending on a 600 ship navy might be in conflict. Instead, Bush signed off on the *Seawolf* class of nuclear submarines (this was after the collapse of the Soviet Union) and continued laying keels for additional super-carrier task forces that included the ostentatious and gratuitous naming of two new carriers: *Ronald Reagan* and the *George H.W. Bush*. Not bad for loading up on debt....

There's nothing wrong with people wanting to get rich. Rich people admit openly that they want more. That is human nature. I've written before about how we evolved as hoarding, thieving organisms in order that our tribes should survive. But those aspects of humanity are ignored in supply-side economics; the hoarders will ALWAYS hoard at the expense of others. There can be NO "trickle down" because it is against human nature to share the wealth. Laws and regulations must do this. It may seem like a subtle point, but there is a difference between sharing and charity. Those societies that do neither usually end up in revolution and insurrection.

We are currently experiencing a political agony that is pulling in two directions: continued adherence to failed experiments (supply-side) and more progressive era practices (higher taxes for the rich) that were in place during strong economic growth for everyone including the middle classes. The outcome of these "experiments" will once again prove or disprove which theory is best suited for the U.S. version of capitalism.

Will the hoarders win and keep funneling money to the upper 1% of the richest, or will more egalitarian types shift us toward improving the lives and opportunities for those not so blessed by inherited or earned great fortunes?

I don't have anything against rich people getting richer. My concerns are for those people who just want to work toward improving their lot and seeing that they CAN enjoy the American dream without breaking the law or the bank.

I wish this "laboratory" wasn't so messy.

The Mirror that Tells the Truth

My very good friend and I played golf the other day. He lives in a very nice, well-to-do neighborhood in our area. The conversation over lunch drifted toward voting and politics, two of my favorite room-clearing subjects. My friend told me of neighbors of his who absolutely despise Rick Perry's "work" as governor of Texas; but they voted for him anyway because they couldn't possibly vote for a Democrat. I asked the rhetorical question, "Why?" The answer we both knew was: "Because a Democrat belongs to the same party as…."that man" in the White House."

The logic here, such as it is, seems to follow that anybody associated with the party of "that man" must be bad. Our President has accomplished much to save our nation from the economic collapse left him by at least the previous administration and probably from contributions by other administrations going back to St. Ronald (Reagan), the "Supply-Sider". He has recently shown us that he can make difficult, politically risky decisions to do what he said he'd do: capture or kill the world's #1 terrorist. He showed his leadership and mettle by ordering it done. He had the confidence in our specially trained military and intelligence communities that performed magnificently no matter what the right wing whiners have said since.

So, what's the problem with "that man" in the White House and, by extension, his political party that drives so many people to vote for politicians and a party who are clearly against their own self-interest? Most of our citizens of every political stripe care deeply about the education of our children, health care for our sick, needy and elderly, assistance for our destitute and chronically unemployed and fairness in most things not connected to money. Why, then, do they continually vote for issues and candidates who are mediocre at best and plain stupid at worst while ignoring people and issues that are clearly more favorable to the majority of Americans?

Leonard Pitts wrote a piece printed in the May 5, 2011 Austin American-Statesman that presents a probable answer to the above questions. The title says it all: *Presidenting While Black.* The article goes into the depth of the human mind regarding inherent and embedded bias in each of us. Our prejudices manifest themselves in many ways even when our mouths are moving and our fingers are prancing across a keyboard saying we aren't prejudiced. But our prejudices remain.

Barack Obama is half-white American and half-African American. I wrote about the trials and tribulations of the first black major league baseball players. Our President is undergoing the same "experience" of being the first not-completely-white President.

Pitts goes on to inform us that we don't publicize our bigotry or prejudices, but we have them anyway. Some ultra-conservative political parties insist they don't have a racist agenda, but many of their members gleefully send out cartoons depicting our President as an African witch doctor or as some "Step 'n Fetch It" character. It is true that these party doctrines and policy statements require that its members refrain from anything smacking of racial depiction, but I have personally received material from some claiming membership and seen other material from them that are clearly prejudicial in nature toward our President.

The recent "birther" nonsense and the alarming statistic that shows that some 30% of Americans believe Barack Obama is not an American citizen by birth, tell me that many of our people are not being honest with themselves. They keep looking for ways to deny that we have a not-entirely-white President elected by the majority of the electorate. Their personal mirrors are either wavy or cracked. Otherwise, how could they cling to the code words and the indirect attacks on our President with such tenacity? Prejudices are hard to overcome, but overcome them we must if for no other reason than to stop making fools of ourselves.

Without the prejudices mentioned in this column, we might have elected a real governor in Texas with citizen skills and statesmanship. We might even have put people in our state legislature and our federal government who represent us for what we are and need instead of some other, less noble agenda. So make sure you look in the mirror of your truth before going to vote in the next election.

Learning the Hard Way

Something I never really expected from writing this column was the amount of positive feedback I have received from many in my community. It is comforting to know that there are people who have learned their civics lessons well and are able to see application of real principles in a working society. Indeed, I have learned much from this feedback about those individual lessons such that they corroborate my sometimes pointed opinions of those who still live in their own world.

I understand that we have special places in our minds, but what I mean is that people exhibit various levels of understanding about how their communities are supposed to work, their state's workings, what the Constitution means and how the Federal government conducts the business of running the country. I have found that those who have a high understanding of these things tend not to fear government, but rather work toward making it better for the society as a whole. They think, as do I, that a well-run government peopled by representatives who have the greater good as their main philosophical position will "raise all boats" such that we all have better, more interesting lives.

This school of thinking was originated with the New Deal of Franklin Roosevelt and its pursuit of Keynesian economics. Government investment in concert with private business built this country into the magnificent land of opportunity it became since World War II. Banks and taxes were well-regulated to prevent chicanery and greed from ruining a good thing for the people. The government seeded many projects and research that gave stupendous opportunities to smart businesses to make pots of money while marketing the best quality product mix in the world.

Then there are those who think that government shouldn't be involved with business and that free market enterprise will take care of everything. History has shown us that this hands-off philosophy lets the dark sides of capitalism and human nature loose and causes the working classes to suffer while the rich reap huge benefits. In fact, this approach to running our country almost ran it into the ground – twice. The first time was called the Great Depression when government sat back and watched 25% of our workforce go hungry while waiting for those free market pressures to kick in. They didn't. When your consumers don't have any money to buy things, cash flow to everyone stops. That's why the wealth of the nation plunged to dark depths in 1929.

We have seen a resurgence of the unproven theory of supply-side economics. Even though its authors won Nobel Prizes for it, it has never yielded anything like its predicted outcomes due to factors that weren't included in the theory or its experimental trials: human greed and avarice.

During the Reagan administration "trickle down" economics was attempted. De-regulation of sound banking rules along with a massive tax cut served to push the country into a huge $6 trillion deficit. "Never mind." said the supply-siders. "Free market enterprise will fix this." It didn't. Raising taxes did. Somebody finally realized that the government needed revenue to pay for things that benefitted the people of the nation and provided job opportunities.

The Bush II administration tired it again along with even more banking deregulation and caused the Great Recession. The Tea Party grew out of the side of this failed experiment in conservative politics and is wreaking havoc on the Republican Party.

The Tea Party types want to cut more taxes for those who can afford them and reduce more government spending for those who need it the most. They think the Constitution was hand-written specifically for their interpretation without a Bill of Rights, without the ability to tax and without the ability to control runaway financial misbehavior. They say they want to take their country back. But clearly they do not know to where it should go or from where it came. Those little tidbits of history lessons are inconvenient truths for those who haven't yet learned what a society of all the people is.

I wonder how hard the lessons will have to be before those extremist fringes understand that the economic and social programs that work are meant for them as well. Floating all boats isn't meant to be a selfish statement.

Let Facts Decide the Issue

Gamblers try to beat the odds in order to get a payday. The professionals know when to leave the table, fold the hand and walk away. The amateurs or the gambling addicts stay until they lose it all. The issue of global warming and the dependence on fossil fuels plays this game with the people of the industrialized world. Some are betting on the COME that their dreams will come true and the human actions regarding the burning of fossil fuel will NOT tax the planet's ability to sustain our form of life on it. Others see the potential danger of staying at the table too long; the table being the massive consumption of those fuels and the wastes the burning of them leaves behind.

The United States, for example, has only 20% of the world's population, but uses almost half of the fossil fuels dug, pumped or scraped from the Earth. We produce, therefore, the most waste from that consumption than any other country on Earth and several combined. China and India are the two most populous nations on Earth at over 1 billion people each. Their industries are just emerging and their consumer societies just beginning to feel the pull of modern, Western luxury items. Add to that the fact that the United States exhibits the lowest percent of efficiency (energy in vs. work out) per unit of fuel in the world at about 35%. Most of Europe operates their fuel consumption at above 75%. Perhaps the worst part is that that 65% of the energy derived from burning fossil fuels is given off as heat; not heat for buildings or homes, but heat into the atmosphere. The Department of Energy will be happy to corroborate that with charts and graphs.

The next part of the equation worldwide is the exhaust resulting from burning hydrocarbons, aka fossil fuels. Our atmosphere is made up of about 79% nitrogen and 18% oxygen. The other 2% contains, carbon dioxide, water vapor and a few inert gasses. When local conditions change by excessive burning of hydrocarbons, oxygen is consumed and carbon compounds are given off upsetting the "typical" balance of gasses. Often overlooked are the oxides of nitrogen that are also part of the exhaust. These gasses contribute greatly to that orange air blanket known as *SMOG*. That word used to be an acronym for "smoke and fog" in combination. Now *smog* is part of the lexicon of human existence.

The first well drilled specifically for finding oil was the Drake well near Titusville, PA in 1859. The ability to extract "rock oil" made the kerosene market explode with excellent lighting oil for the east coast. The internal combustion engine followed soon after and we all know how that turned out. The point is that it has now been 152 years since that well was drilled and scientists are predicting that we have discovered all the oil there is and we will consume it all by the middle of this century. It took over 200 *million* years for oil to form during a unique period in our Earth's geological history, but in less than 200 years our rapacious use of petroleum will exhaust that resource by our voluminous, wanton and often irresponsible use of it.

Well, you might say, "So, what if the scientists and the geologists and the oil drillers are wrong and there is much more oil left?" That may be true. The *Deepwater Horizon* disaster showed the world how hard, expensive and dangerous it is to extract those last precious drops from deep in the Earth's crust. The point *here,* though, is that the oil will be gone some day. No professional gambler is going to bet that it won't be exhausted, nor will he bet on the day it becomes impossible to obtain.

This subject has fascinated me ever since my graduate school days at San Diego State University during the debate over the Alaska pipeline and its environmental impact. The National Geographic Society has been covering environmental issues like this for the 50 years I've been reading it. In 2008, for example they committed an entire issue to global warming and man's cause-effect relationship. The graph that pegged my attention meter was the one where the measured rate of atmospheric carbon dioxide and the increase in global atmospheric temperature over the last 20 years of measurement tracked almost exactly the same slope. That means that the volume of CO_2 is directly related to the warming of the atmosphere.

Subsequent issues of that journal like the one in June, 2010 on Greenland keep documenting the progress of this phenomenon. The summary statement from this and other articles is that the ice sheets and glaciers on the planet are dwindling – *rapidly*. In fact since 2006 until this year, the rate of shrinking of ice sheets and the speed with which glaciers are moving has increased geometrically; that means at an increasing rate.

Is this just more "alarmist" rhetoric? Not really. These phenomena are being measured in great detail by scientists around the world who are cooperating to define a potential series of catastrophes that may cause the human condition on Earth to change dramatically. Al Gore caught a lot of flack for his award-winning film, *An Inconvenient Truth.* The facts are that the research presented in that film has been subsequently corroborated and expanded by further, independent research. There will always be naysayers right up until the seawater starts flowing under the doors of their beachside dwellings.

It is difficult to predict what will happen first. Will global warming melt all the sea ice in the Arctic Ocean while all the major glaciers are reduced to slivers before we run out of oil and stop burning coal? Or will our atmosphere become so polluted and the ozone layer so depleted from that pollution that we will be forced to live in protective shelters to avoid ultra-violet light destruction of our skin cells?

One of the major accelerators to global warming is the liberation of methane from the millions of acres of permafrost in Siberia and the Northern Territories of Canada. As the permafrost freezes later and thaws earlier, more methane will be released. Methane, aka natural gas, is also a greenhouse gas that traps more of the sun's heat, thus accelerating an already difficult problem. Somehow, I don't see it as practical for energy companies to be out there on the soggy tundra trying to suck up the methane as it comes bubbling out of the ground.

If the reader assumes that what I say here is correct and that scientific fact overwhelmingly verifies that the global warming phenomenon exacerbated by human activity is real, then the question begs: "What do we do about it?"

First, the Earth is not going to die. What will change with rising seas are the addresses for about 60% of the world's people who live within flooding range of predicted levels. The growing ranges for various crops will also change as climates change; winter wheat will be grown in northern Canada instead of Nebraska, for example. Littoral zones (those zones of life defined by certain altitude/weather/climate restrictions) on mountains will change more dramatically than they already are today. Animals and plants will face extinction in greater numbers than ever. Plankton in the oceans that now produce about 40% of our fresh oxygen will be affected in a negative way; the water will simply be too warm and saline for them. New species may evolve rapidly to offset this, but there will be a die off. Reefs will die due to warmer waters and changing currents that will cut off their food sources. Weather will be affected by changing ocean and air currents such that previously fertile regions will either become deserts or water inundated marshes.

These predictions come from computer modeling of changes in global temperatures from the graphs extended into the near future. Forget the disaster movie scenarios. The climate will change slowly, but inevitably. It may take a century to reach the end point of this trend before a reversal begins.

Next, we the people of Earth must change our priorities in a complex way, but beginning with the simplest of tenets. We simply must stop reproducing so rapidly. Population growth drives everything else in the phenomenon of resource depletion and its link to global warming. As arable land dwindles, growing sufficient food to support a growing human population generates a graph where the descending calories available line crosses the ascending calories required line and mass starvation begins. That sounds like an avoidable outcome to me.

Developing alternative energy programs and implementing those that work best must become our number one priority. That subject will consume another essay entirely. While we still have the fuel to operate societies and industries under current conditions, we have to use that time to make fossil fuels obsolete. Sooner or later, they will be gone. That's a sure bet.

Progress Without Discomfort

A quote from the historical icon, Frederick Douglass in 1857 seems most appropriate even today:

The whole history of the progress of human liberty shows that all concessions yet made to her august claims have been born of struggle....If there is no struggle there is no progress. Those who profess to favor freedom and yet deprecate agitation, are men who want crops without plowing up the ground. They want rain without thunder and lightning.

Clearly there is much "agitation" in today's political discourse, and maybe that's how it should be. As uncomfortable as it is to participate in debate with someone who does not share your ideas or philosophies, it is debate that must happen in order for us to live together. Those who try to fracture this bond of debate do more harm to the fabric of this country than any of us who participate in it do, irrespective of its intensity.

Douglass, of course, was talking about the coming conflict between cultures where debate stopped and violence replaced it. It took nearly 700,000 dead Americans and hundreds of thousands more injured in war to figure out that debate might be a little less damaging than open hostility. Many of us debate and argue with one another to the point of disgust and name calling and all the rest, but no muskets are loaded, or knives drawn. We already fought a civil war, we don't need another.

I would like to imagine that the progress Douglass talked about can still occur today. Progress means to go forward, not backward. Progress, I think, means to go forward as a nation and not as a collection of little ideological cells of self-absorbed righteousness. As much as politicians and their handlers want to divide us up into those little pieces, we must resist. We must continue the debate no matter what.

Karl Rove may go down in history as being the most significant character in dividing post-WW II Americans into ideological camps that are not only diametrically opposed to one another politically, but incapable of holding intelligent conversation or debate. How did he do that? Why did he do that? He did it by telling his employers to never admit a mistake, always blame the opponent for things gone wrong and always attack your opponent to constantly keep him/her on the defensive. This strategy created anger and divisiveness that Rove's candidate exploited to garner votes. They didn't care that it turned voters off and minimized the poll turnout; indeed, fewer voters meant more likely outcomes in their favor.

The best example today of this strategy gone to extremes is the Tea Party/Birther movement. The angry, self-centered "policy" of this group is now trumping (pun intended) reasonable discourse even from the Rove-schooled Republicans who keep playing to their "base". From everything I read, this base is becoming increasingly radicalized and is attempting to make success seem like failure, good people seem like fools and positive attempts to do good seem like evil. What kind of base are we talking about here? What sort of society wants to be built on a base like that?

Some will chastise those of us who engage in spirited debate because it makes them uncomfortable. I refer to Douglass's speech again, and submit: Maybe this is how we salvage positive outcomes from the mess left us by Rove's tactics. If someone is uncomfortable with it, then maybe they should find other ways to express their ideas. If someone only wants to debate and argue in ways that nurture their comfort then they should do that. The point is that progress must be made. If it is not, we will slide back to the banal prejudices and uncivilized hatred that marked our time as an uncivil society in the 19th century.

We will probably never all agree on exactly how things should be, but we should all strive to find ways for our individual ideas to find points of agreement and overlap. Sometimes, in order to do that, we must have moments of discomfort with one another including with those we love and respect. That is human nature. That is how progress is made. This is the 21st century, not the 19th.

It Isn't That Hard to Understand

There remains a strange concept that keeps permeating our political debate: *government does not create jobs*.   Nothing could be further from the truth. If people studied how we became the most powerful and richest nation on Earth with the best infrastructure, public education and health care system the world had ever seen, they would recognize the very significant role government played. Instead, our "learning" is centered around "gotcha" political games predicated on a gross error in judgment and philosophy.

I am talking, of course, about the false theory of Milton Friedman: *Supply Side Economics*. The Reagan administration embraced this faulty theory because big business and big banking told it to. One has to go no further than Reagan's chief of staff, Donald Regan, the former CEO of Merrill-Lynch who fronted this ideology and "managed" the Reagan administration's actions to implement it.

President Reagan kept telling us that the government is not the solution, but the problem. What that really meant, as we've come to see, is that it was corporate/banking America that wanted government out of their lives so they could do what capitalists do: Do whatever it takes to maximize economic profit and gain at the expense of human and non-human resources until they were exhausted.

To return to the theme about government creating jobs one only has to look at the history of our infrastructure. No President before Reagan suggested anything like "government does not create jobs", because it was government sponsoring private enterprise that got everything built. Even though most of our past Presidential administrations were in bed with corporate/banking America, there was work to do and money to be made from the taxpayer...lots of money. The country also reaped huge infrastructure growth and development. Today, by contrast, money is made for the sake of making money, not infrastructure.

The fact is our government creates jobs that matter to the country as a whole. From the discovery and settling (some would say invasion)of the Western Hemisphere by European immigrants to the purchase of the Louisiana, Gadsden (southern Arizona) and Alaska territories, the building of ports, subways, railroads, aqueducts, canals, bridges, water and sewer systems, public sanitation departments, paving city streets, roads and highways to the creation of our public school and university system, the electrical grid, the internet and the space program, nothing would have happened if not for a political decision...and that without these projects we would still be riding horses and throwing our sewage out our windows.

Yes, Edison invented the light bulb but the streets would still be dark if some politicians had not voted to allocate taxes to install street lights. All these projects were built by the private sector, but that was after the government had put up the tax dollars to start the project. Government, through taxation, creates the opportunity from which the private sector profits. That is the American economic formula for progress! And that is how we will rebuild our present economy: by creating jobs that matter.

In my infinite naiveté I expect most people to see that the jobs pump must be periodically primed for our nation to make progress in order to lead the world in so many areas. I expect my fellow Americans to see that the minute some entity like education or health care is turned over to private enterprise it starts faltering and becomes mediocre or elitist or corrupted for the sake of profit and at the expense of the people. Certain things that serve our citizens and our nation simply shouldn't be for profit. There are countless other projects, like rebuilding our inner cities, which will provide plenty of profit for our capitalists and bankers.

All we need to have is enough leadership in government to prime the CORRECT pump by ending our preoccupation with wars, and directing our tax money to rebuilding that infrastructure that has been allowed to crumble under the boots of greed and special interests. Civil distress in this country is a function of poverty. As our people become poorer, our national vigor and world leadership turns right toward the trash heap of history.

There are plenty of opportunities for all boats to be raised. In our class-stratified society, the seas may not all be the same altitude or depth, but everyone will have a boat that floats and enough to eat so that rowing it won't be much of a hardship. Our working people deserve the chance to row their own boats.

Defining the Meaning of Words – Again

Once again the question of motive in defining common words used, abused and thrown about as if their meanings were understood has recently struck me. Having read an opinion piece that blamed our faltering education system on liberal policies through the ages plus meeting some very interesting progressive thinkers pushes me once again to try making sense of social lexicon.

The word "conservative", for example, is defined in the dictionary as preserving what is and resisting making changes. Fine. The word "progressive", sometimes used synonymously with the word "liberal", is defined as "...favoring or advocating progress, change, improvement or reform as opposed to wishing to maintain things as they are..." So, when I hear or read about conservatives talking about reform, as in education reform, I wonder what they mean. It is especially puzzling when I look around at the way the rest of the world does things and see progress in just about every social area that keeps pushing our country further and further behind.

Our conservatives, for example, wish to maintain a health care system that gouges the individual or family by continuously raising premiums and cutting services all the while resisting universal, single-payer health care. Since the insurance companies have put a stranglehold on our health care our national health has plummeted from 1st in the world to the high 20s in quality. The rest of the world, by the way, practices some form of universal, single-payer health care. None of them are perfect, but none of them are 29th in citizen health either.

Our conservatives want to "reform" public education by making it private. Our progressives want to "reform" public education by exacerbating the stupidity of *No Child Left Behind* with *Race to the Top*. These two approaches are all about money, not education quality. So, while our ideologies squabble over which "reform" will work best for their constituencies, our children's education keeps dropping compared to the rest of the world.

The rest of the world recruits teachers from the top tiers of college graduates, pays their would-be teachers for earning their license or certificate, sends their kids to school for over 200 days per year and pays their teachers and administrators salaries equivalent to their equally educated peers. None of these systems are perfect, but most of them aren't 35th in student knowledge and falling either.

My main question here is, "Why do we keep doing things that don't improve our quality of life, while adhering to one ideology or another?" Obviously, being conservative and maintaining what is in place is a loser. Trying to make progress toward improved health care or education seems stalled by political agenda, corruption in government and funding of ideas that clearly don't work. Why is that the way it is in this great country of innovation and ideas? It seems neither conservatives nor progressives are living up to their defined job descriptions.

We can't seem to get it that cost accountants working for insurance companies are not qualified to make medical decisions, never mind setting the scale of cost.

While we remain in this intellectual limbo, the rest of the world laughs at us and takes their citizens to higher levels of health and education. Does any activist conservative or progressive ever wonder how our children will compete in the global economy? Do they ask why our people are sicker and dumber than the rest of the civilized world? Do they fail to understand that healthy, educated people are infinitely more productive than what our systems are churning out?

Maybe this is the nation that conservatives want. If, by definition, they revere the absence of change and progress, then why is the rest of the world changing and progressing? Do our conservatives know something they don't?

Maybe this is the nation progressives want. If, by definition, they revere progress, why aren't we making any, or as much as we should to keep up with the rest of the world?

Maybe conservatives and progressives have become so enamored of their opposition to one another that any changes involve too much political risk such that we become the paralyzed giant, the has-been country that never wants to be great again.

I think all who read this understand the definition of the word "mediocre".

The Ashes of a Victory Pyre

After the November mid-term elections, when only 48% of registered voters did their civic duty, there was great celebration among the Republican/Tea Party members who felt the "people spoke" on their behalf. Well, actually the margin of victory in the most lopsided races was about 25 points. Not bad. But when you look at the percentage of those eligible to vote, it constitutes a slightly less noble number like 35% of the eligible voters voted for the "winners". The average margin of victory was about 6 points. That means that about 18% of the eligible voters picked the winners. Keep in mind that 30% of eligible voters remain unregistered. I guess they figure the rest of us will take good care of them.

That brings me to the theme of this column: taking care of our fellow citizen. Earlier this year I wrote a column listing where Texas ranks among other states in taking care of its citizens and its children. In most of those categories, Texas ranks in the bottom 5 among the 50 states. In some key areas like per capita spending on our citizens' welfare, Texas is last. Texas is also last in high school diplomas, but first in high school dropouts. So, naturally, the voters of Texas re-elected a governor and legislators to perpetuate this condition...except for this:

The new legislature wants to cut even more from our social services and education budget items. Our San Antonio Representative, Joaquin Castro summed it up perfectly when he said, "So you've got to ask yourself...at what point is this budget akin to asking an anorexic person to lose more weight?" The title of my earlier article was "Cuts to Make Last Place Worse".

Everyone knows that actions have consequences. The small government, cut spending crowd will soon be sifting through the ashes of their victory pyre looking for reasons why things went so wrong. They will look for reasons, other than their own short-sightedness, for the exodus from Texas of educated families who want to educate their children in high quality schools. The property values of neighborhoods in areas of high pollution will continue to plummet thus cheapening the value of the entire state. Good paying jobs will follow the educated workforce to other states and Rick Perry's "miracle" will be seen for what it has always been: a short-term scam to keep his pals in corporate/banking Texas happy. It will be seen as an overdone hairdo: all fluff and no substance, or as another Texas aphorism goes: He's all hat and no cattle. Over 75% of the jobs recently created in Texas were minimum wage, another category where Texas leads the nation.

When a society guts its social services and stops adequately educating its children, allows its poor to suffer even more and brags about it, most historians will tell you that the bell is tolling that society's last days. As former Texas Lt. Governor Bill Hobby said, "If you wanted to destroy an enemy, you would do what the Republicans are doing in Texas."

If you read the paper or watch the news you will find no conversation about increasing revenues for the state budget balancing act. The Texas legislature simply ignores raising revenue as a partial solution to reducing the $23 billion deficit. That deficit is the consequence of bad government with bad tax policies and runaway bureaucracy. It only took 12 years for things to get this bad. As the late Molly Ivins once said about the Texas legislature being "the national laboratory for bad government", this latest election has produced a wretched experiment in irresponsible government.

The joining of the republicans with the Tea Party and the "birthers", and all the rest of the right wing loopy-ness, has created the perfect storm for not only bad government but a peek into the hearts and souls of the citizens who elected those people into office. Why in the world would our good and true citizens keep electing people and voting for policies that are against their best interests and against the best interests of the state as a whole? What is so attractive about being last with its citizens' welfare? How can Texans be proud of having the highest high school dropout rate in the nation?

The victory pyre in November must surely have consumed reason and vision in the victors, because they cannot or will not see, in the ashes of that fire, what impact their partisan actions will have on the short-term and long-term consequences for the people of Texas.

What's Really Important? Hint: It isn't Ultra-Conservatism.

The history of capitalism in the United States shows painful and turbulent evolution. The turbulence comes from the relationship between labor and the hierarchy of businessmen who exert influence on national policy, the interpretation of law and demands on the government.

After the Civil War, a resurgence of capitalism created huge labor and product markets – especially in the North. The South's industrial infrastructure was in shambles, and freed slaves streamed North to readily available jobs. At first glance, one might think that this was good for everyone. It was not.

Northern white workers coming home from the war needed to work to support their families who had had to suffer economic hardships similar to, but not as horrible as their Southern counterparts. Businesses, however, only cared about how little they could pay for labor. The blacks, of course, took jobs for fractions of what white workers would ask. The inevitable friction between the races in the North was exacerbated by white labor disaffection with the business and industry leaders who did what any capitalists normally do.

Over the next decades, the *Populist* movement was replaced by the *Socialist* movement that led up to and included the First World War. These two eras had commonality in that working conditions for labor were utterly dreadful on today's standards. No laws existed to protect workers from employer whimsy and abuse. No laws existed to protect workers from unsafe working environments. No laws existed that defined a limited work day or week. The wages were draconian in their parsimony.

Imagine, for example, sending your 12 year old son to work in a sweatshop of the late 19th century. He would have to work 60-70 hour weeks for less than a dollar a day. Factory women were treated about the same for about the same wages. Woe unto the employee who got sick or was late for work. If they weren't fired outright, they were often whipped by foremen.

Meanwhile, corporations and businesses were reaping record profits and all the while trying to expand markets. The Spanish-American War, for example was fought primarily to gain control over more resources and larger markets for the surplus of goods being produced by American human and mechanical labor. The drive for profit was limitless and relentless. American Imperialism was necessary to slake the thirst of American capitalism during this time.

When labor organized and revolted, the conservatives' position was almost exclusively repressive. The first amendment right to assembly was ignored as hired militia and mercenaries were sent in to disrupt and disperse organized labor. The result, of course, was violence. Hundreds of men, women and children were gunned down in our streets and fields because they didn't want to be indentured servants to the company store. The conservative governments actually allowed Federal troops to go to the rescue of businesses as the revolts and strikes grew more frequent and more intense.

As America lurched toward anarchy and open class warfare, conservative administrations began the painful process of reform. They saw that without reform there would indeed be another revolution. One of the salient events that spurred this move was the Ludlow Massacre in Colorado. Dozens of men, women and children were shot and burned to death because they wanted to be paid in U.S. currency and have safe working conditions for themselves. Instead, the Rockefeller Trust paid the salaries of the Colorado National Guard to break the strike by any means possible. Killing strikers became a normal occurrence sponsored by corporate/banking America. This was the price of reform for how capitalism would exist in the United States.

This history reflects but a sample of what conservative philosophy did in the name of profit. Today, the conservatives want to overturn many of the laws of the reforms that so many people died for. Ultra-conservatives want to return to the time when government did not interfere at all with how businesses were run. There is even a movement in Missouri to allow school children to skip school so they can go to work.

Ultra-conservative movements are clearly out of date and fail to understand that certain kinds of bells cannot be un-rung. The bell of fairness and caring about our fellow citizens cannot and will not be un-rung by the people who think they want to "take their country back."

"...not because they are easy..."

This phrase was part of the speech President John F. Kennedy gave in May of 1961 announcing our goal of putting men on the moon "and returning them safely to the Earth". He said he wanted to do this "and the other things, not because they are easy, but because they are hard"! What, exactly, did he mean by that?

It is now 50 years since he made that speech and the challenge to do the hard things has never been greater than it is today. In the 60s, the political will was supported by the people because true leadership and statesmanship was at the helm of the United States. Kennedy portrayed greatness in leadership no President has exhibited since. Why not?

Kennedy challenged us all to do something great. Today, it's all about getting elected and making your opponent look the fool or worse. Today, it's about raising so much money for elections that it would fund one of the moon missions. Today, it's about the divisions of political ideologies that would make those elder statesmen hang their heads in sadness and disgust. Nobody is out there challenging the American people to do something great. Why not?

I say again: It is about getting elected. Then, it is about getting re-elected. The takeover of the media by corporate moguls who want to slant the "news" toward their best interests is normal for today's capitalists. That's what they do no matter whether it's the media or making ashtrays. It's their exclusive interests that matter most. The people of America have come to expect nothing more from their representatives, and when a bold leader appears he/she is shredded by the other party or parties such that their message becomes part of the background noise associated with selling papers, magazines and air time. We are, therefore, strangling our own voices of hope, change and leadership by constant sniping and arrogance that says the other side can't possibly be right. We create complex lie programs to justify our positions. When somebody does tell the truth, nobody seems to have a basis for understanding it.

George H.W. Bush collected Karl Rove, Lee Atwater and Roger Ailes to his bosom back in the 70s. He used them throughout his political career because they advanced not only his career, but those of other Texans who joined this cabal: Dick Armey, Phil Gramm and Tom DeLay. I use the term *Texas Mafia* for these guys. As a group, this lot has had more to do with driving wedges between political ideologies than all the pro- and anti-slavery groups did in the 1840s and 1850s, in my opinion. The results today might end up being the same as those of the 1860s. I left out George W. Bush because he was merely the final experiment in political demagoguery by this group of miscreants. You'll notice that once his strings were cut in 2008, he disappeared into the back of the closet of discarded puppets.

What we do have today is as daunting a challenge as we had in 1961. We are tasked with "binding up our wounds" from 30-some years of divisiveness and fomented anger at one another. We must do it, of course, because if we don't we are certain to enter a period of

91

anarchy, rebellion and spiritual rending the likes of which we haven't seen since the beginning of the 20th century.

Corporate/banking America cannot be allowed to wag the dog of our governments any longer. They are literally fighting us, the ordinary citizens, for the heart and soul of our country. The deregulation laws are, to corporate/banking America, the economic bogeyman that they keep trying to tell us they are so they can just make more profit. That's what capitalists do. I'm not slighting them for that. My concerns are for the working classes of people in this country who will be either the fodder for a new wave of indentured servitude, or will be bypassed altogether as their jobs, careers and the rest of our manufacturing base are shipped to places with the cheapest labor and the fewest safety and environmental controls.

We must stop this trend not because it is easy, but because it is hard.

A Reason to Yell!

Sometimes it is hard to keep promises to oneself. I promised myself I would remain calm, not get angry, stop ranting and become nicer to be around. Then I started watching the news and reading the paper. I threw open the window and stuck my head out and yelled, "I'm mad as hell and I'm not going to take it anymore!!!"

Those of you who have seen the movie *Network* know what this means. How in the world do TV networks justify airing whole segments on Congressman Wiener's ...well, you know what? How do high paid millionaire news show hosts get away with ranting about twits and twerps in a presidential race that is 18 months away? Iowa caucus? Who cares? Do you really care which of the announced republican candidates wants your money to stand up there and make a fool of him or herself?

People I really care about have asked me to run for office so our local Republican "representatives" wouldn't go unopposed on the ballot. After thinking it over, I began to wonder if they really liked me. I make a fool of myself easily enough let alone running a political campaign around here as a democrat. I didn't see much redemption in losing 72%-28% to any of these local people in state government. I've met them, and I don't have the stomach to lose anything to them, not even a golf game.

Why is the media so in love with Sarah Palin? Can't they see that she is playing them like a violin? If they do, how do we the people justify spending time and money following this rubbish. The next time I hear that squeaky voice tell us about American values and hard work, I'm going to lose my most recent meal for sure. And our people are lapping this stuff up like cats do cream! Why?

The Republicans in the House of Representatives are telling our President that unless he favors cutting *trillions* of dollars from the Federal budget, they won't vote for raising the debt ceiling. For those of you not familiar with this issue, if we don't raise our debt ceiling, we will start defaulting on our international loans. You know, like Greece is about to do. Maybe that's the republican way of playing "gotcha" with China since they hold most of our notes. Oh, and another thing: the universal currency in the *whole world* is the U.S. dollar. What do you suppose will happen to the economies in the rest of the *whole world* when we stop paying our bills? Can you say, GREAT DEPRESSION II?

Not one single sentence coming from the republicans talks about raising revenue by taxing the richest. "Oh no." they say. "This is the wrong time to raise taxes." Was it the right time to cut taxes for the rich while fighting two wars off the books, while giving away trillions to Big Pharma?

They go on to say, "Well, businesses won't create jobs because of the uncertainty with the budget." Who do you think is creating that uncertainty by being unremittingly against taxing corporate/banking America, by closing loopholes and raising the income rate to pre-Bush II tax levels? Corporate/banking America is sitting on trillions of dollars of capital and they are *uncertain?* Uncertain about what? How much cash do you need to start feeling certain about something?

Well, I feel *certain* that as long as people keep electing these very corrupt people to public office, we are looking at the edge of the abyss of failure as a society. We have NEVER defaulted on our loans before and the Republicans are playing chicken with our country over an agenda that has no upside. How did we let this happen?

Oh. Right. Fifty-two percent of our registered voters stayed home because they were turned off by the ugliness of our political process, just like those who got elected hoped they would. With 30% of our eligible citizens not registered to vote what else should we expect BUT corruption and incompetence from BOTH major parties and certainly from the minor ones.

O.K. That's my yell. I'll go back to being calm.

More Reasons for Finding Statesmen and Women

Much of this column comes from the one published by Thomas Friedman in the New York Times. It illustrates what short-term thinking and an utter lack of statesmanship coupled with mindless fear can do to foreign relations. Nothing better defends the policies toward Israel and the Middle East of our current administration than this analysis.

Friedman's recent trip to the area resulted in several findings that show how thoughtless, outdated and craven the previous administration's policies were after 11 September 2001. He includes the Arab states, America and Israel —" all of whom have deeper holes than ever to dig out of thanks to the Bin Laden decade, 2001 to 2011, and all of whom have less political authority than ever to make the hard decisions needed to get out of the holes.

"In 2001, Osama bin Laden attacked the World Trade Center and the Pentagon. Just a few months later, in 2002, the U.N. issued the '*Arab Human Development Report*,' which described the very pathologies that produced Al Qaeda and prescribed remedies for overcoming them. The report, written by Arab experts, said the Arab states suffered from three huge deficits: a deficit of freedom and respect for human rights as the bases of good governance, a deficit of knowledge in the form of decent schooling and a deficit of women's empowerment."

So, naturally, our administration ignored the report just as they ignored the open handed offers from our European allies. Macho replaced intelligence and statesmanship. As long as these Arab leaders arrested, interrogated and held the Islamic militants in their societies and eliminated them as a threat to us, we looked away from the repressiveness of their regimes.

What happened in the Middle Eastern nations now struggling for freedom were repression of dissent and the installation of cronies or relatives of the current leaders as successors.

"As the Arab leaders choked their people that much tighter, along came Facebook, Twitter and cellphone cameras, which enabled those people to share grievances, organize rebellions, lose their fear and expose their leaders: 'Smile, your brutality is on Candid Camera.'"

The bad news is that now the newly liberated Arab states are in deeper, more desperate economic situations as well as having greatly reduced infrastructure that includes educating their citizens. Reforms will be more painful and difficult than they should have been.

Egypt, for example, has a political vacuum and will have to endure an IMF-like austerity program that cuts government spending when they need it most to rebuild that infrastructure.

"In America, President George W. Bush used the post-9/11 economic dip to push through a second tax cut we could not afford. He followed that with a Medicare prescription drug entitlement we cannot afford and started two wars in the wake of 9/11 without raising taxes to pay for them — all at a time when we should have been saving money in anticipation of the baby boomers' imminent retirement. As such, our nation's fiscal hole is deeper than ever and republicans and democrats, rather than coming together and generating the political authority needed for us to take our castor oil to compensate for our binge, are just demonizing one another."

The trust so desperately needed in that region and in our country, Friedman suggests, is broken just at a time when it is most needed. How will an Israeli-Palestinian peace process be brokered by anybody who isn't trusted by either party, for example?

Barack Obama did the right thing in killing bin Laden. He did the right thing in NOT invading Libya. His administration is *trying* sort out how and where we can help to rebuild the trust lost by the previous 10 years of bumbling, self-centered foreign policy. The oxymoron is intended. So, the next time you hear the whining and ranting from right wing pundits or presidential wannabes, remember what all that "compassionate conservatism" really meant to us and to our "friends" in the Middle East and elsewhere.

If you must vote for someone other than Barack Obama next year, at least try to pick somebody with some statesmanship and real leadership ability instead of him or her being just another puppet of corporate/banking lobbyists. We indeed did just that when we elected Barack Obama in 2008.

My Favorite Liberal: You Know Him by Another Name

Some of my editorial colleagues often use scripture in their columns to make points of morals, character and politics. Since conservatives are so often identified with Christianity and the purity of the soul these days I thought I'd take a try at pointing out that even here in central Texas, there are liberals afoot with good, solid values too. Indeed, some of us actually practice what we believe in. Let me begin by introducing some profound words.

The Spirit of the Lord is upon me, because he hath anointed me to preach the gospel to the poor; ...to set at liberty them that are bruised.

That is a pretty daunting job description for my favorite liberal. Well, with this task in hand, he set forth to fulfill the wishes of his "employer".

Blessed be ye poor: For yours is the kingdom of God. Blessed are ye, when men shall hate you, and when they shall separate you from their company, and shall reproach you, and cast you out your name as evil...

Woe unto you that are rich, for ye have received your consolation. Woe unto you that are full, for ye shall hunger.

I'm guessing here that my liberal friend was actually trying to get the attention of the rich while showing some compassion for those in need. Why would he do that? Aren't the rich and powerful and well-fed supposed to do the ruling? Well, he goes on to offer the rich guys some hope:

...and if you do good to them which do good to you, what thank have ye for sinners also do even the same, and if ye lend to them of whom ye hope to receive, what thank have ye for sinners also lend to sinners, to receive as much again. Love ye your enemies, and do good, and lend, hoping for nothing again; and your reward shall be great; and ye shall be the children of the Highest. Be ye therefore merciful as your Father also is merciful.

You can't help but like where this is going. It seems that my friend is saying it's O.K. to share the wealth, or as we say in 2011: Redistribute the wealth. Today, there are many who go absolutely bonkers about that concept. I hear things like: "Well, we're giving entitlements to people for WHAT they are instead of WHO they are." Why do I detect a coded intent here? My good liberal friend here wouldn't think of saying that, would he? No, instead he'd say something like:

Judge not, and ye shall not be judged. Condemn not, and ye shall not be condemned. Forgive and ye shall be forgiven.

Give, and it shall be given unto you; good measure...

Wow. It sounds like if we are generous to our fellow man we will reap benefits from our generosity; kind of like an investment. I may be stretching the point, but don't our social services in government attempt to do that on a large, organized scale? Doesn't paying something out of our earnings allow our government to help those in need, those who are infirm, or those who desire to uplift themselves through education? Oh sure, there are those who will try to cheat and fiddle this generosity. For those people and for those who speak of love and respect of others, yet do things counter to those admissions, my friend has more words:

But he that heareth, and doeth not, is like a man that without a foundation built a house upon the earth, against which a stream did beat vehemently, and immediately it fell, and the ruin of that house was great.

I keep reading and hearing about deficits and budgets and entitlement cuts and how we have to all sacrifice to balance the budget. I hear little of the things that my favorite liberal says about people in these discussions taking place all about us. Have we come to the point where money is more important than people? Do those who think this way relate to any of the teachings of my favorite liberal, or do they have a different teacher who preaches the gospel of mammon and nothing else?

The Bill of Rights – II

On January 11, 1944, President Franklin D. Roosevelt made his last State of the Union speech from the White House. In it he introduced some things that have since been forgotten or addressed piecemeal. The war, his failing health and, ultimately, his death obscured the key features of this speech which I attempt to resurrect here.

Roosevelt's argument was that the "political rights" guaranteed by the constitution and the Bill of Rights had "proved inadequate to assure us equality in the pursuit of happiness.

In our day these economic truths have become accepted as self-evident. We have accepted, so to speak, a second Bill of Rights under which a new basis of security and prosperity can be established for all—regardless of station, race, or creed.

Among these are:

The right to a useful and remunerative job in the industries or shops or farms or mines of the nation;

The right to earn enough to provide adequate food and clothing and recreation;

The right of every farmer to raise and sell his products at a return which will give him and his family a decent living;

The right of every businessman, large and small, to trade in an atmosphere of freedom from unfair competition and domination by monopolies at home or abroad;

The right of every family to a decent home;

The right to adequate medical care and the opportunity to achieve and enjoy good health;

The right to adequate protection from the economic fears of old age, sickness, accident, and unemployment;

The right to a good education.

All of these rights spell security. And after this war is won we must be prepared to move forward, in the implementation of these rights, to new goals of human happiness and well-being.

America's own rightful place in the world depends in large part upon how fully these and similar rights have been carried into practice for all our citizens.

For unless there is security here at home there cannot be lasting peace in the world."

The countries that adopted these rights after the war were Germany, Italy and Japan, our former foes. Their new constitutions included all these rights and they are in practice today. We, on the other hand, fought with each other like dogs over bones to limit these rights or disguise them as part of capitalistic competition. The huge fight over health care is the perfect example of how we lost sight of pursuing happiness for ALL our citizens because we couldn't see short-tem profit in it.

Health care SHOULD be a right, not a commodity to be fought over, profited from and doled out by some leaders who have political agendas. Education is another example of how we have confused capitalism's imperatives with the needs of our people to best support long-term wealth. Education SHOULD be a right, not a commodity to be fought over, profited from and doled out by some leaders who have political agendas. Is our profit motive so addictive that we can't even heal and educate our people unless they have enough money? Those who think profit for everything is the only way to go for these two basic social needs should not include the word *morality* in their lexicon.

We claim to be the richest nation on Earth yet we have the highest rate of poverty in the industrialized world, rank in the high 20th percentile in health care and the low 30th percentile in educating our children. These numbers tell me that for-profit everything is NOT the pursuit of happiness or *"promoting the general welfare"* of our citizens. We also have the highest incarceration rate in the world, irrespective of national economic status, and that prison population is 75% illiterate. Am I the only one connecting the dots here?

I think we should dedicate our economic pursuits to this New Bill of Rights and away from wars that have no purpose except to drain our resources and kill our soldiers. In pursuit of these rights I envision a nation that liberates itself from foreign oil, cleanses itself both physically and morally and fulfills the dreams of our founding fathers – who are so often misunderstood – such that we can become the true beacon of idealistic democracy that was their original intent.

Against Our Better Interests

While recently attending a forum of highly educated, dedicated citizens to discuss all things American, one of the "show stopper" questions was, "Why do so many people keep voting for people and things that are against their best interests?" Several answers were bandied about, but no consensus emerged as none of them made sense in view of the overall political and social environment.

When it was my turn I mentioned that the demographics where I live are roughly 72% republican and 28% democrat or independent. I pointed out that in the November election, almost 75% of Republicans voted straight ticket while only about 28% of democrats did so. It would seem, therefore, that democrats are more discerning in their voting habits while republicans just punch a ticket no matter who is running for office as long as they are republican.

We pondered that issue for a while and determined that the republican way of doing business was to do what you are told, ask few questions and just follow orders. This is where it gets weird. The population around my readership tends to be older and more inclined to health and retirement financial concerns, yet they voted for representation that advocates cutting health care, retirement and hospice care for those very people. Why would they do that?

The majority of people I know of every political persuasion think it is good for our country and the world if we educate our children at a world class level. Yet, most Republicans voted for representation that advocates cutting education funding and making it still more difficult to educate the inner city children as well. Why would they do that?

Most republicans advocate and vote for representation that extends the Bush II tax cuts of 2001. On this 10th anniversary of the first Bush-era tax cuts, the following should be noted:

These tax cuts allowed disproportionate benefits for those at the top of the earnings distribution, widening income inequality.

• In 2010, the top 1% of earners (tax filers making over $645,000) received 38% of the breaks in the 2001-08 tax changes; 55% of the tax breaks went to the top 10% of earners (those making over $170,000).

• The top 0.1% of earners (those making over $3 million) received an average tax cut of roughly $520,000, more than 450 times larger than the share received by an average middle-income family.

• These cuts included lower tax rates on capital gains and dividends, elimination of both the personal exemption phase-out and the limitation on itemized deductions, lower marginal rates for the top two tax brackets, and lower estate tax rates and an increase in the estate tax exemption.

The surplus inherited by Bush was used to fund this cut, but the cuts kept coming and the revenues went the other way. Most republicans are NOT in the top 1% (but almost all of the top 1% are republicans), so why would they vote for cuts that actually hurt their smaller businesses or financial positions? By the way, jobs disappeared coincident with these tax cuts.

The Gramm-Leah-Bliley bill of 1999 overturned the Glass-Steagall Act that prevented banks from speculating with depositor money and allowed the bad/exotic loan bubble that precipitated this recession as it did the Great Depression in 1929. Why did so many people vote for representation that would do this to their own portfolios?

So, here we are precariously balanced on the precipice of fiscal disaster because too many people voted against their own best interests and, as a result against the best interests of the country. How did we get to this place? How could our small electorate (only 48% of registered voters voted in November while 30% remain unregistered) be so naïve to be snookered by politicians and their parties that are clearly working for interests other than those of our citizens?

Getting rid of the straight ticket option would greatly enhance voter "intelligence" by making them pay attention to each candidate. Also, imagine what kind of candidates would emerge from our communities if they knew that 75% of the people would vote. Imagine what kind of candidates we would see on the slates if corporate/banking money was NOT allowed into the election process. Doing these two things might just be in our own best interest.

When the Message is Clear...

Some who see themselves as self-ordained experts insist that climate change/global warming is alarmist rubbish coming from liberals and progressives and should be ignored. They might want to look at reality. In the 7 June 2011, *N.Y. Times'* Thomas Friedman discusses realities that are seen as facts in his column titled *The Earth is Full*, because they've been observed and measured.

He asks a rhetorical question: "You really do have to wonder whether a few years from now we'll look back at the first decade of the 21st century — when food prices spiked, energy prices soared, world population surged, tornados plowed through cities, floods and droughts set records, populations were displaced and governments were threatened by the confluence of it all — and ask ourselves: What were we thinking? How did we not panic when the evidence was so obvious that we'd crossed some growth/climate/natural resource/population redlines all at once?"

"The only answer can be denial," argues Paul Gilding, the veteran Australian environmentalist-entrepreneur. "When you are surrounded by something so big that requires you to change everything about the way you think and see the world, then denial is the natural response. But the longer we wait, the bigger the response required."

Denial. This is a convenient behavior for easing pain, discomfort and realities we don't want to face. We do this all the time. We deny the passing of a good friend or relative because it hurts so much. We deny that our kids are continuing to receive less than a world class education because it means that we have abdicated our responsibility as parents and the control of our government; we have let it control us. That really hurts. It hurts both conservatives and progressives. We hate to admit we're wrong about anything. I know this first hand. I become very upset when I'm proven wrong. First, I deny it, then I do my own research and when it verifies that I made a mistake, I humbly and grudgingly admit it. My denial is just as wrong-headed as the original mistake.

Gilding cites work by the *Global Footprint Network*, an alliance of scientists, which calculates how many "planet Earths" we need to sustain our current growth rates. *G.F.N.* says we are currently growing at a rate that is using up the Earth's resources far faster than they can be sustainably replenished, thus threatening our future. Right now, global growth is using about 1.5 Earths. "Having only one planet makes this a rather significant problem," says Gilding.

Specific examples of what the future looks like include countries that are currently in total denial and seen in hard-pressed places like Sana, Yemen. Fresh water must be trucked in because the city is at 150% of the carrying capacity that the Earth can provide. This is not science fiction. This is what happens when human growth and the system of nature hit the wall at once.

Humans are a rapacious lot. We consume and waste like there's no tomorrow. Well, someday, there WILL be no tomorrow. We'll have reproduced and eaten ourselves right out of a perfectly good planet. Americans, it seems, are the leaders in waste and consumption, but there are many other examples where the mad dash for financial gain (an abstraction) comes at the expense of the planet's resources (reality). Most of Europe is above 75% efficient in their use of energy, while the United States, no longer the most technically advanced country in the world operates at about 25% efficiency. Most of our wasted energy escapes as heat. Europe traps that heat of combustion and uses it for a variety of things including generating more electricity.

From the early 1960s to around 2000, Japan led the world in importing plywood. They paid countries like Indonesia, having vast tracts of tropical forest, to cut their trees and make plywood. Why? They used plywood in vast quantities to make forms for concrete while building their infrastructure after WW II. Today, China is doing the same thing with lumber from Indonesia, Africa and South America. Thankfully, countries like Brazil saw that their most precious resource were those tropical forests that were being denuded to the tune of one Rhode Island per year.

Denying the inevitable exhaustion of resources as our human population rolls past 7 billion is not only foolhardy, but will inevitably cause our extinction.

Oliver Stone is a genius at creating provocative theories and graphically presenting them such that the viewing audience is compelled to at least consider the possibility that a conspiracy was/is afoot. His conspiracy masterpiece, *JFK* took us all for a ride through the dark caverns of unanswered and unanswerable questions about that tragic day in Dallas and what surrounded it. Many, many books have been written about this event, the first of which, *Rush to Judgment* by Mark Lane, is still considered by many to be the definitive work for JFK conspiracy theorists.

Why are we so fascinated by conspiracies? Is it because we don't want to believe the worst in human behavior? Can't we, in this open democracy, accept behind the scenes intrigue in our own country that is so prevalent in European history? Yet, when a conspiracy is exposed as true, our greatest fears, or vicarious needs are satisfied and we look for more. In my lifetime I have seen many events that, if not uncovered completely, would have been conspiracy theories for decades after. The *Watergate* events come to mind. The Nixon administration unhinged itself trying to cover up the shenanigans it was pulling on the American people, for example.

The "outing" of those involved in the Iran-Contra debacle during the Reagan administration showed how close we came to being more cloak and dagger than peace and assistance. Then, we had to understand the times.... After all, we still had this wrenching fear of communism taking over the world irrespective of the demise of the Soviet Union and the non-player status of China in the 1980s.

The list goes on where potential academy award winning conspiracy movies could have emerged from just our own government's dealings with world events. The Gulf of Tonkin incidents that kicked off our full involvement in Viet Nam were lies. But we didn't know that until much later. Conspiracy to commit deceit on the American people, anyone? Imagine the final scenes when LBJ finally realizes he's been railroaded into this war by the military-industrial complex and big oil. Our hearts would break.

A really juicy conspiracy script might have been written about the Bush family beginning with Poppy Bush's dealings with the Saudi families that included the bin Ladens. I can just hear the script writers' keyboards singing as they explain how the Saudis perhaps rescued Neil Bush from the Silverado Savings & Loan scandal. Now, the Bush family had plenty of money to do this, but it would be unseemly to have a President covering up his son's misdeeds. In the end, the taxpayers paid for the bad and illegal loan restitution while the Bush family and their friends in the newly de-regulated banking and loan businesses got richer. Too bad those darned journalists kicked over most of the rocks and spoiled a perfectly good conspiracy.

There still may be a few good ones out there, because there certainly are a lot of questions yet to be answered truthfully. Why, for example, didn't George the First finish the job in Iraq in 1990-1? Was he afraid that Saddam would have torched ALL the oil wells in his country and leave none for us to exploit? I mean, we just smacked his whole army except for his elite guard units in 100 hours! From what I was told by veterans of that war, the Iraqi soldiers and citizens were begging us to oust Saddam. It may have been the first time in our history when we limited our military action because of a U.N. resolution. Why?

Now there are theories floating around about the Bush II administration knowing and abetting the 9/11/01 horrors to promote yet another war. It could be a great movie script too. Why, for example, did we invade Iraq when we already knew that Osama bin Laden (that name again) was in Afghanistan cozying up with the Taliban? The American people were flat-out lied to – again. Those lies seem to have a nasty habit of creating conspiracy theories.

These conspiracies make me crazier than I already am. I hate them! Won't somebody please tell the truth and we can put these darned things to rest?

Energy and the Environment

For what they're worth, here are some ideas presented as a plan on both a large and small scale. Certainly, some small plans can end up being part of larger ones as in the "another brick in the wall" process.

1. Reduce military spending by $200 billion per year and invest that money into alternative automobile and truck fuels such as electric and bio-diesel. Converting current ethanol production to bio-diesel is relatively simple in that the ethanol factories become grain or seed squeezing factories. The diesel engine runs very well on safflower, soy, pecan and other naturally occurring, renewable oils. Some of the corn used in ethanol production can be sold to Mexico and other countries facing food crises brought on by growing corn for ethanol. The land that is converted to soy, safflower or other oil producing crops will be reinvigorated and more productive. Bio-diesel can also be used for jet fuel thus helping the airlines control fuel costs and easing the carbon footprint of the planes' exhaust.

2. This is a kind of 5-year plan that could become a normal part of our future business and cultural climate. I intend for that trillion dollars to be invested in item #1 above as well as those below.

3. More research is needed to develop the existing technology into cost-effective production of electron storage devices that are long-lasting, light weight and easily/quickly re-charged. The Swiss, I believe, are working on these kinds of batteries using more exotic materials. If there will be a market to achieve economies of scale, investing in vehicles powered by these devices that replace gasoline powered vehicles will produce the momentum to get off of Arab oil imports.

4. Every new building and home should be required to have alternative energy collection technology such as solar panels for electricity and hot water built into their original designs. When this technology is part of the original design, it is MUCH cheaper to employ than to retrofit later. Included in these requirements must be power off detectors and switches that prevent careless use of energy when it's not needed: motion sensors, person-in-the-room sensing, appliance or device usage sensor (just like our computers have) would be built into controlling devices that will also control temperature based on the owners'/managers' requirements. In other words, we would be developing smart homes. Think of the jobs created by companies building these devices. Subsidizing home and apartment building owners to employ this technology is just part of the plan.

5. Establish a nation-wide plastic collection program that includes reducing the plastic chemically (there are bacteria that attack plastic) and taking those by-products for reuse or some other outcome like medicine and drugs. Eliminate plastic shopping bags everywhere and replace them with bags made of reusable materials. The merchants will be subsidized for getting rid of plastic, but will also make a profit by selling reusable bags with their advertising on them.

6. Return to the use of glass, refundable bottles and jugs for beverages, cosmetics and cleaners. Certainly aluminum can re-cycling must be continued; can recycling is the poster child for successful social action. Plastic wraps for everything from potato chip bags to crackers to breakfast food must be replaced with renewable material like waxed paper…just like the "old days". New waxes can be as impermeable to air and water as plastic and greatly reduce the permanent footprint of non-recycled trash.

7. Take non-recyclable trash from dumps and compress it into blocks that can be used for road beds or building foundations. Sealed and coated trash bricks can also be used for other building materials including factory or office floors. Getting that crap out of our ground water drainage will certainly help reduce the micro-doses of carcinogens that seep into drinking water. Crushed and compressed automobiles, once all the chemicals are removed, would make perfectly good foundation blocks as well. The metals in junk cars could also be re-cycled via steel and aluminum smelting. Imagine how happy all the junk dealers will be when they get paid nicely to have the junk they can't sell hauled off.

8. During the wars of the 20th century people were asked to donate their surplus pots and pans to make war materiel. These "volunteer" collection programs were hugely successful. Why don't we institute them again, but this time go after not only surplus metal, but plastics as well. Put those plastics into the re-cycling process industry that will boom happily along with making nothing but profits for new businesses and putting people to work.

9. Require that all cafeterias and restaurants collect their unused food and garbage and either compost it themselves, or create large, community compost businesses that will make and sell it back to gardeners and, on a larger scale, to farmers. This would replace chemical fertilizers to a great extent and once again help ground water purity. For the amount of food we waste as a nation, this should be a no-brainer for successful enterprise. Help out households with subsidies if they either contribute their organic trash to this program or use it themselves in their own

gardens. Keep in mind that the less frequently trucks have to transport produce to market, or the fewer trips the trash trucks make, the less will be the demand for motor fuel of whatever type.

10. Giant wind farms may seem like a good idea, but the resources required to build and maintain them are significant. Instead, have each household and town/city put small wind generators on their building and property to generate electricity for each unit. That will take pressure off of the "grid" and save fuel for power plants. Similarly, large scale solar collection farms should be supplemented with unit solar collection as mentioned earlier. Cities, towns and villages could also paint all their rooftops white to reflect sunlight and thus abet global warming a little while saving money and electricity on air-conditioning.

11. Used tires should be collected massively, shredded and used for road and walking surfaces in as many places as possible. State highway departments should be required to purchase their road materials from private companies that have been created to make it. Shredded tires are currently being used for artificial athletic fields, so we already have the technology to employ this basic idea and only need to apply it to the creation of long-lasting roads.

12. The "just-in-time" philosophy of delivery of goods and materials to stores and factories must be re-examined in light of the cost of transportation. Currently, stores and factories are taxed on their stored and warehoused materials inventories. To avoid those taxes and reduce real estate costs for storage space and equipment, "just-in-time" brings material to the shelves or the assembly operation at its point of use only as needed. This requires many more transportation trips and thus adds to the overall carbon footprint associated with transportation. In view of declining petro-fuel availability, the cost break for warehousing will become paramount; indeed, tax codes could be re-written to eliminate the "just-in-time" motive. I realize that perishable items will still require more frequent deliveries, but long shelf-life items can be delivered at longer intervals. Furthermore, abandoned stores and warehouses can be reactivated to help store inventory.

13. Increase the incentives to use more natural fibers and materials for clothes and furniture. By growing our own materials for clothing and furniture, we might just revive the millinery industries and make money in the process. When oil is burned to ship oil from oil-producing countries to other countries to make clothing and furniture made of plastics, then more oil is burned to ship it here for consumption, the opportunity for huge oil usage reductions is available here. Yes, huge, oil burning ships will go out of business, but if they can be converted to utilize wind

sails to supplement diesel, then shipping costs for other goods could be reduced as well. Without "just-in-time" rapid transport across oceans won't be as critical. Furthermore, our clothing and furniture businesses could once again become competitive since we'll be growing our own materials.

This 13 step program is just a series of suggestions from an old industrial engineer and scientist who knows a bit about the environment and the impacts of waste, overuse and short-term thinking. When the oil is gone, it will be gone forever. That is a guaranteed fact. Meantime, while it is still cheap enough and we haven't fought any major wars to secure its sources, we have to move toward the day when oil will not be part of our activities on this planet. Furthermore, the human population continues to grow at an exponential rate thus putting more strains on food production, pollution of food producing and human preservation entities like fresh, clean drinking water, to say nothing about the rapidly increasing rate of oil and oil product consumption. I hate to say it, but pollution may be incidental to starvation.

Uncontrolled consumption will always be with us. That problem is exacerbated by the human propensity to waste and discard mindless of the consequences. The flip side is that humans are also the most adaptable species the planet has ever seen. That ability to adapt is, ironically, being thwarted by economic factors such as greed and sales incentives for things nobody needs. So, my proposals intend to exploit those human frailties and turn real fixes to our problems into business opportunities which will, undoubtedly, create even more opportunities. The key is to embed *consequence technology* such that negative outcomes can be turned onto themselves and direct a positive outcome for the species and the planet.

Tickling the Dragon's Tail

During the early phases of nuclear physics that led to the first chain reaction and the building of the first atomic weapons, the scientists would let masses of fissionable materials approach criticality so they could measure the amount of particle and energy emissions. This was ghoulishly labeled "tickling the dragon's tail." Since these scientists hadn't seen a full blown fission event, they were kind of whistling through the graveyard of new discoveries, some of which often failed with catastrophic results.

The United States Congress of 2011 is tickling the tail of another kind of dragon. Unfortunately, the members of this Congress share almost nothing with the scientists in Chicago and Los Alamos in the 1940s, least of all intelligent decision making. One chief difference between these two groups is that the scientists in the 1940s were motivated by a world war wherein our enemies might invent the ultimate weapon before we did and win that war. Today's Congress is dealing with mere economics. I don't mean to imply that the economic situation of today is inconsequential, just that cataclysmic destruction of a people and a way of life aren't as much in the forefront today as they were in 1944...or are they?

In 1944 the highest income tax bracket reached toward 90%. Today, it is 35%, or less than half of what it was when we were engaged in a world war involving millions of service men and women. Our population in 1944 was about 135 million. Today it is over 310 million. In 1944 we the people of the United States were prepared to pay virtually anything to prevent real tyranny and despotism to invade our land. Today, we are willing to pay virtually nothing to prevent the greed of a few from destroying not only our economy but the economies of those other countries who actually think we have the best economic system.

Indeed, some consider our massive economy as much luck as innovation and hard work. We were the only major economy that escaped unscathed during that world war and we happily exploited all the trade and commerce possibilities left open by the collapse of the British and Japanese Empires. We just got richer while the rest of the world struggled to rebuild their infrastructure.

In spite of the yowling by corporate/banking America and their conservative employees operating our government, the United States has the lowest per capita tax burden of any industrialized nation. Yes, it's true that corporate taxes are among the highest in the world, but the exemptions from paying those taxes are so many that our major corporate earners actually get refunds from the IRS. If you own a corporate jet and fly clients in it, you can deduct the cost of the flights and the depreciation of the aircraft from your taxes. If you are a major oil company, you publish reports showing us that you are making record profits every quarter while at the same time receiving publicly funded subsidies. If you produce ethanol as an alternative energy or grow the corn to feed that misguided and remarkably inefficient enterprise, you receive tax breaks, subsidies and exemptions to ensure that you are profitable.

The dragon being tickled today is world-wide economic collapse and meltdown. With the unbelievably unyielding positions of congressional Republicans, we are at the brink of defaulting on trillions of dollars of loans from other major economies. Why? Because, say the republicans and their red-headed stepchild, the Tea Party, by not raising the debt ceiling we will stop going further into debt. I wonder how many home owners understand this concept, especially when the lien holders raise interest rates on defaulted loans to recover their lost interest from those bad loans. The international finance community will do this to ALL loans once the confidence in the U.S. system of government and finance is ruined by our own stupidity and greed.

The Obama administration is offering a couple trillion dollars in spending cuts over the next decade or so, but the Republicans, as has been their wont for 2½ years, are saying NO to any revenue increases. They refuse to even talk about closing loopholes in the tax code that favor the rich, raising high-end income taxes to pre-Bush levels and cutting off subsidies for already profitable American businesses.

What if this economic dragon is not ticklish and feels pain instead? How loudly will the dragon roar and how far will the flames reach when the collapse of the world economy is at hand?

How could we have possibly elected such utterly mindless "representatives" when the solutions are so simple? Let the dragon sleep. Electing government that is not beholden to corporate/banking America would be a nice way to tip-toe around that beast and actually make solid, fiscally sound and economically just decisions. What a concept!

The Moral Bankruptcy of our Politics

By the time this column makes it to the presses, we will know whether or not the United States of America will survive as the dominant economy in the world, whether or not it will pay its bills, or whether or not its people will have enough to eat. From the unbelievable theater of our national political environment comes enough doubt and uncertainty to make these situations part of the conversation about our future as a society and a nation.

We are witnessing the most absurd of times regarding the fiber of this country's moral fabric and its social cohesion. Every pot of soup needs stirring, but the stirring up of the political pot has brought to the surface a vile, stinking mixture of bad loans, bad ideas, bad people and bad resolutions. There is no upside. The reason is that finance and money have usurped the human being as our national substance. Worse, the management of our money and the people who are grasping for every penny is beyond avarice. Our government isn't so much out of control regarding its spending habits as it is mindlessly pushing itself into oblivion for the sake of the few who control most of the wealth in our country. There is no consideration for the masses of Americans who do not enjoy the ridiculous wealth of the top 1%-2%.

When the top 400 richest can control our national politics, we have failed as a democratic republic. It's just a matter of time before anarchy becomes the mood of the day. The money changers have indeed entered the temple and they are destroying everything they touch. The world economy has become their ultimate playground and they are not minding who gets destroyed on the altar of profit. This is moral bankruptcy on a grand scale the likes of which the world has never seen.

The pitiful few from a right-wing extremist organization have taken over a major political party to the extent that the parent party must do its will. The Tea Party is the virus, like HIV, that has entered the republican system to destroy it from within. In so doing, they are ready to sacrifice all of us on the other alter covered with fiscal blood, the balanced budget. They are willing to expose their imbecility for all to see by insisting that the world's economy must enter a season of panic that will shatter the lives of billions of people. Why would they do this?

Angry, selfish people do irrational things. When enough angry, selfish people congregate and find a flashpoint for a common theme, they form a political party; in this case it's the Tea Party. In 1933 it was the National Socialist Party. The Tea Party is American, the National Socialists were German. Both parties are extremely right wing in their practices, philosophy and goals. They intend to destroy government to gain power themselves. Today, the Tea Party and others, exhibit a pathological dislike for Barack Obama. That "dislike" is irrational and counterproductive to the activities of this government. The Tea Party doesn't even understand that this President has given more away to conservatives than any other Democratic President in history. Yet, they detest him still. Why? National Socialism gave the world Adolf Hitler. Who will the Tea Party foist upon us, Michele Bachmann? Newt Gingrich?

My suggestion that our government and its politics are morally bankrupt regarding the economy and our national compass is not easy to say. I'm defending no political party; everyone seems to be playing the game. I'm suggesting that we, as a nation, have taken our eye off the ball. When we stopped voting in large numbers, we let the foxes into the hen house. When we allowed corporate money to pick our candidates and kept re-electing the refuse that this produced, we aimed the gun at our own feet. When we allowed the banks to run wild with our money and their inherent greed, we set the stage for social and fiscal moral corruption. We the people have only ourselves to blame. We did not pay enough attention. The result of that sloth is the moral breakdown of those who presume to govern, but are actually only in it for the money.

Promises, Polls and Mandates

If you've been reading this column for any amount of time you've seen my attempts to quantify inequalities, lies, misappropriations and misrepresentations of the truth. Take for example the election of a famous president who won in a "landslide" by garnering a whopping 51.6% of the popular vote. His two opponents received 41.7% and 6.7% respectively. The kicker is that only 54% of the eligible voters voted. The winner in a landslide was none other than Ronald Reagan in 1980. A full 27% of the eligible voters picked Reagan. This is a landslide.

The above trend continued. Reagan was re-elected in 1984 with a stunning 29% of the eligible voters selecting the "great communicator". This time only 50% of voters turned out. In 1988, George H.W. Bush beat Mike Dukakis with 54% of the vote, or 27% of the eligible vote. Voters stayed home in droves again.

Maybe there are reasons why so many voters avoid the ballot box. The people said they would pay more in taxes if it helped the destitute and the poor. The political parties said, "No, they wouldn't". In 1990, a poll in Boston found that 54% of voters would pay more to clean up the environment. The political parties declined to pursue this. Also in 1990, a *Wall Street Journal* poll found that 84% of voters favored a surtax on millionaires. The political parties avoided that issue altogether. In 1989 a Harris/Harvard poll showed that 61% of Americans favored a Canadian style, single-payer national health care system. We still don't have that. In fact, just last year over 60% of Americans again asked for a public option for their health care. That hit the caucus floor and was not included in what has become known as *Obamacare.*

In 1992, a survey by the Gordon Black Corporation found that 59% of all voters wanted a 50% reduction in defense spending. No cuts were suggested by either party. A *New York Times*/CBS poll in 1992 found that 64% of voters favored the government helping the poor. In 1987, 62% of Americans favored guaranteed food and shelter for needy people. None of these voters' requests were addressed by either major political party.

More recently, over 60% of American voters favored stricter gun laws and regulations on guns. Instead the NRA and other gun lobbies convinced our "elected" officials to relax gun laws even more.

There is a pattern here where the people are not being heard by the politicians they elect to office to represent *them*! Is it any wonder they stay home election day? They know that this isn't really a government of, by and for the people anymore. So if not, what?

Pundits of every stripe and even people who think clearly say much the same thing: The lobby is the thing. An opinion or a desire or a policy that the people want has to be presented or "pitched" through some mechanism that uses large sums of money as its lubricant. If this is the case, where does the money come from to do this lobbying on a daily basis? Ah, yes. The corporations and the banks, that's where the money is.

We mustn't forget the vaunted Supreme Court that allowed corporate/banking America to act as individual people so they could contribute unlimited funds to any candidate they wanted without telling anybody. This "ruling" applied to unions too, but since unions only represent about 13% of the workforce of mostly middle class workers, the field seems tipped in the corporate direction.

The poor voter: the politicians don't listen to him or her. The polls don't matter. They don't have the money or the time to lobby. Their candidates sell out to the moneyed interests. Wars keep getting fought against their will while their sons and daughters die for oil and minerals.

I no longer wonder why the voter turnouts are so low. Even with the great surge of voter interest during the 2008 cycle, it seems that business has returned to normal, except this time the economic situation for the average American is dire. Will that pressure drive more people to the ballot boxes, or will it drive them into the streets or into the offices of their representatives? We'll soon see.

It Took a While...

With my limited capacity to synthesize information and come to reasonably accurate conclusions, it took a while for me to understand some of the questions I've been asking for over a year. I kept asking, for example, why people don't run to the polls to vote in droves. I think I now understand why.

The people have been lied to too many times. They have been ignored too many times. They've had promises broken too many times. They've seen wealth disappear into the highest reaches of society and came to realize that no matter whom or what they voted for, none of it would ever reach them. To the people who learned that their votes really *don't* count, the American dream is a myth. There is no "power in the people" because the capitalists have seen to it that most in the middle classes have just enough to keep them quiet. The poorer classes, as they always have been, are ignored completely.

President Clinton had a golden opportunity to implement universal, single-payer health care that sociologists around the world had been advocating for decades. Even our own Presidents of the early and mid-20th century saw that we had enough wealth as a nation to do this without much trouble. But, no. That would mean that insurance companies and their friends in banking would be cut off from another profit stream. So, that part of the dream died in the gutter of obfuscation and the false fear of the misused words: *socialized medicine.* Never mind that the rest of the industrialized world utilizes this idea to have a healthier populace than we do. It's the profit stream that overcomes common sense, compassion and caring for our fellow citizen.

That brings me to our pre-occupation with guns and violence. We are a warring nation. Always have been, always will be. In fact, we've only been at peace for about 10% of the time we've been a nation. That brief period between the World Wars was probably our most pacifist period in the second half of our history, but labor strife and class warfare inside our own borders kept the flame alive. It finally dawned on me that we don't like each other very much. We're also scared to death of one another. There's always someone out there ready to do us in or steal our pearl necklace. We must, therefore, be armed to the teeth to "prevent" such horrors. Has anyone asked who the "bad guys" are? Why are they bad? The bad guys tend to be bad because they have no hope, no interests, no education, no health and most definitely no wealth. That's a stereotype, I know, especially when we consider the theft occurring on Wall Street.

The absence of hope, education, opportunity and adventure leaves an intelligent person at a loss to fulfill their lives and have some purpose. Everyone has to have purpose, don't they? If you are one of those lost souls who have not had adequate parenting or mentoring or instruction, you are going to look for alternative lifestyles. This realization led me to understand why we have a multi-billion dollar illegal drug situation in this country. No wonder we are a nation that pursues chemical enhancements, both legal and otherwise, to either cover the pain of our hopelessness, or alter the reality of our physical pain, humiliation or sense of lack of purpose.

I get it now. Over the last 40 years, the wealth of this country, by way of broken promises to the people, the altered tax laws that favor corporations, the defused regulations on banks, the perverted tax laws that eliminate fairness, has skyrocketed upward to the top 1%-2% of the wealthiest individuals – and they want more. With the banks and corporations sitting on trillions of dollars that are not putting people to work while they complain they aren't receiving yet more favor from our government and government with only a few remaining moral and ethical elected souls, disgust and a loss of national pride seems inevitable.

I wonder when enough of those citizens in the bottom 98% will have had their fill of this kind of a greed-oriented land and take a stand and do something dramatic. I also get it that when the top 2% have taken all the wealth, there won't be any wealth for anyone else. What will happen then? Stay tuned.

This column was written several months before the "Occupy" movements started sweeping the nation. I guess I'm getting my answers to the questions I've been asking in this book.

Masts on the Horizon

Our earliest memories of realizing that the Earth was round probably came from a geography lesson that demonstrated that the first things we'd see when a ship was coming toward us while at sea would be the masts, not the whole ship. We would test this using the big globe in the classroom. We got it. This example, of course, came from ancient seafarers who witnessed this phenomenon daily.

To carry this further, many ships affixed banners and flags to their mastheads for all to see. Sometimes the approaching ship had to come fairly close before a seaman could read what was on those banners.

I think our ship of state should be scanning the horizons for the masts of an approaching ship fitted and sailed by the people of the United States of America. In this case, the ship of state includes the Congress and the Supreme Court as well as the President. They should carefully place their telescope to their eyes so they can read the banners of the people's ship as soon as possible.

The people's ship on the horizon is not a man-o-war, but merely a galleon of hope and hard work, crewed by those who seek truth and fairness. Furthermore, the crew and its leaders are prepared to alert the ship of state in the distance that as the distance grows less, the message about to be delivered will become more evident.

As with previous times of civil unrest, the people are about to speak their minds based on their desires and dissatisfaction with the direction the ship of state is sailing. It is nearing the time when the writing on the banners will be revealed as one word: *rebellion*. The people of the United States rebelled against British rule when it became oppressive enough to stifle the concept of freedom. Southern Americans rebelled and seceded from a union of states when they misunderstood the meaning of the Constitution and ignored the lessons of the Bible and common decency. That rebellion was abetted by the intransigence of northern industrialists and abolitionists. Both of these rebellions were bloody, open conflicts of arms.

The ending of one of those rebellions saw a new nation born from strife with a Constitution that attempted to allow a democratic republic to flourish and grow with the times and events. The second rebellion ended with a re-unification of the truncated nation with new amendments to the Constitution that tried to eliminate the causes for the rebellion. Both of these periods were very messy, contentious and upsetting to peace and tranquility. The "pursuit of happiness" was merely a glimmer for most Americans during these times.

The looming crisis of government we see today is quite different. Extremism is attempting to dominate reason. Greed is trying to usurp the voice from the majority of the people for its own ends. Leadership is virtually absent in our government; statesmanship being replaced with shrill and childish partisanship that serves no one except those who have sponsored the people masquerading as legislators and political leaders, corporate/banking America.

Recent elections have served to do little to change this atmosphere of dysfunction. The only "new blood" in Congress has come in the form of a radical fringe that is controlling a major political party in spite of its minority status. The Tea Party actually filled the void of leadership on the political right. While politicians from both ends of the spectrum lined up at the corporate trough, the Tea Party actually served different masters: their constituents.

Wouldn't it be great to return to those days when mainstream political parties actually answered to their constituents? Maybe it's time to invoke Article V of the Constitution that allows the people and Congress to make and implement amendments to the Constitution. Times have surely changed since the last one as corporate/banking America has usurped the election process and rendered the people's voices mute. Perhaps it's time to remove corporate money from the selection and election processes. Perhaps it is time to remove the legalized bribery, aka lobbying, from our political system. We're allowed to do that. The Constitution gives us that right and power.

If we do this, maybe the banners on the masthead of the people's ship will read: "We are in charge of responsible government."

Signs of Revolution

As of this date, 26 July, 2011, our national government has covered itself with ignominy by refusing to compromise on a national budget while holding the nation's economy and potentially the world's hostage by not raising our debt ceiling. The resulting default on our loans invites international chaos.

Eric Cantor, a representative from Virginia, has repeatedly refused to consider raising any new revenue to help quell the debt or balance the budget. He, as well as the other republicans, who lead various parts of their party insist that raising revenues by closing tax loopholes and eliminating government subsidies funded by taxpayer money are "new" taxes. They further insist that during an economic downturn, increasing taxes kills jobs. The fact is that most economists who are not on corporate payrolls state otherwise, using history as their support.

It seems to my recollection of history that when our country was in peril, partisan politics took a back seat to necessities to solve our problems and/or defeat our real enemies. Mr. Cantor's action smacks of a major attitude shift in our national fabric. Does his "take my-ball-and-go-home" behavior tell us something more about why we can't solve this economic debacle facing us? There is something sinister about our national government, now, that I've not read about or seen since just before the Civil War.

Let's review a little recent history to see where this cloying anxiety comes from.

1. Ronald Reagan is elected President and hires the CEO of Merrill-Lynch as his Secretary of Treasury, Donald Regan. The administration embraces Milton Friedman's Nobel Prize winning theory of Supply Side Economics and employs Grover Norquist, an ultra-conservative think-tank type to establish new taxation policies that favored the wealthy and the corporations.
2. In 1999, Phil Gramm, with the help from a Republican Congress, overturned the Glass-Steagall Act of 1933 to allow banks to use depositor money to speculate on a wide variety of commodity markets including home mortgages. Their new bill also permitted banks to insure themselves while gutting the Federal Depositor Insurance Corporation.
3. The North American Fair Trade Agreement allows companies to move jobs to Mexico and Central America for lower labor costs.
4. George W. Bush is appointed as President by a Supreme Court's decision to stop recounting votes in Florida from the 2000 presidential election. Al Gore wins the popular vote by a wide margin, but loses the electoral vote to Bush.
5. Bush's economists go to work to employ supply-side economics. First, they cut taxes for the wealthiest citizens, the results of which destroy the surplus from the Clinton years and add roughly $2 trillion to the national debt over the next decade. Second, after the attacks of 11 September 2001, Bush sends troops to Afghanistan to root out Osama bin Laden, the mastermind behind them. Then, while lying to the American people, he orders the invasion of Iraq presumably to eliminate threats from *weapons of mass destruction.*

For the first time in American history the government does not raise taxes to pay for war and indeed further reduces them for the wealthiest people in 2004 adding additional trillions of dollars to our debt. The American people are told to go out and spend on things in order to pay for the wars and the looming deficit.

During this time, the banks are making and selling bad loans at home and abroad. Foreign countries and banks, except Canada, discard sound lending practices and join in the free-for-all of loan packaging and "exotic" schemes to make and hoard mountains of money. Then, a funny thing happened: all those bad loans came due. Almost overnight, the wealth of the entire civilized world dropped precipitously by double-digit trillions of dollars.

This combination of events, of course, precipitated bank failures and the great abstraction, international finance, teetered on the brink of collapse. With the advent of the Great Recession, more debt was incurred by way of unemployment insurance and other safety net program cost jumps.

So who was responsible for these misguided financial disasters? It wasn't the man in the street. It was largely due to our elected officials who either made laws to allow these things to happen, or ignored laws that prevented them from happening or both. The voters, the minority of those eligible who participated, finally realizing that they messed up, returned the House and Senate to Democratic majority control in 2006 then elected an intelligent President in 2008. Why? "Because President George W. Bush cut taxes in the service of his party's ideology, not in response to a groundswell of popular demand — and the bulk of the cuts went to a small, affluent minority. " (Source: Paul Krugman)

Bush chose to invade Iraq because that was something he and his advisers wanted to do, not because Americans were clamoring for war against a regime that had nothing to do with 9/11. In fact, voters were never as solidly behind the war as America's political and pundit elite. This is nothing new, of course. The peoples' desires are lost in the dense fog of politics and finance.

There are those who see the cynical side of these recent times. They see it as a CIA-style government removal-remake exercise like the one they performed in Chile a few decades ago, or in Iran, or in Nicaragua. The process includes making government less functional by cutting revenues for it. Then, a politically based media outlet or outlets tells the people that their government is not being run correctly and only *their* selected candidates can make it happen. Do the terms "starve the beast", or "government IS the problem" sound familiar? How about Fox News saying they are "fair and balanced" then do everything they can to make the Democrats look like the fall guy for all things wrong? Try hard to recall when Fox actually pilloried one of their republican favorites for doing something stupid.

The concept to overthrow a current government is applicable in our political environment and media today: Control what the people see and hear as much as possible, create economic and political chaos, blame the current government for the mess, and convince the public that things will only get better if "their" side is back in power. Sometimes governments are overthrown violently and all sorts of weird results happen; like right-wing fascist dictatorships. These are the tactics of today's Republican Party and have wreaked havoc with the truth and distorted informative facts beyond recognition and relevance. The Tea Party is currently being used as the loud shout of disinformation while it creates more pundit noise to distract the barely aware electorate from hearing anything of reason from the political left.

Much has been written of Karl Rove's and Roger Ailes' influence on the political media and candidate behavior. These guys certainly operate by their own playbook, and that playbook is written like the scenario above.

What about simple accountability? Why are the people who advocated budget-busting policies and wars of choice during the Bush years escaping indictments and inquiries like the Clinton administration had to endure? How can those responsible for the current financial crisis be allowed to pass themselves off as deficit hawks? Where is the media in exposing these misdeeds so that the people see them?

A better answer, perhaps, is that by making up stories about our current predicament that absolve the people who put us in financial jackpots like the one we're in, we end up not learning anything from the mistakes of the past. If we have to go blaming people and holding them accountable, then why don't we do that instead of re-electing them?

The only time, for example, you hear about the "liberally biased" media is when they're uncovering misdeeds from republicans and conservatives. Why is that? Where was this liberally biased media when Bush and company were lying to us about WMDs, taxes and de-regulation? Why aren't Bush and Cheney and Rumsfeld and all the rest under indictment for abuse of government power? Where are today's Woodward and Bernstein to smoke out the liars and thieves and bad guys from the Bush administration and Wall Steet?

Are all these things the seeds of the next revolution? Is this what happens when a real and true democracy is threatened by the power hungry? Even a thumb-through glance at civilizations everywhere show this power grab behavior at whatever cost to be "normal" to the human condition. Is our democratic republic next on the block? Will *We the People....* become just another quaint notion that had its day and retreated until something else came along to replace the relatively unsophisticated style of governance known as despotism?

How will it happen here? What will spark the next revolution? Will it start as a small thing like somebody being evicted from their residence and committing violence against authority thus triggering an outburst of violence from the communities of the oppressed?

Or will the revolution come in the form of a participative democracy. This would be my choice. Allow me to dream: Imagine a society where it was required that each eligible citizen voted. But rather than it being an infringement of a right to dissent, it was seen as a totally patriotic act and promoted as such because every citizen would know how the government worked, who was working it and why decisions were made for *their* benefit. Becoming eligible to vote would be a rite of passage like getting your driver's license. Imagine a society that revered citizen participation in their country's future as much as operating a motor vehicle. Be still my beating heart.

Imagine a society where it was illegal for politicians to receive ANY money from private donors. What if every legitimate campaign was publically funded? Yes, that's right! The political wannabe would have to actually get a significant number of signatures from us, the participants, in order to get on a ballot. So, instead of just pandering to the people with all the money, those wannabes would actually have to meet his/her constituents. Wow! Think of it! You would get to elect someone you knew and met and actually shared ideas with. My heart beats faster still.

Imagine a society with a political structure that made lobbying illegal. Oh, there would be no infringement on the freedom of speech, because citizens would still have the right to petition for having their grievances or wishes heard and addressed. Special interests would have to get the approval of *the people* in order to get their way. Notice that I haven't suggested that we eliminate representative government. That's needed to prevent social chaos as opposed to the graft, deceit, greed and illegal activities of the current system. Imagine what kind of candidates we'd see if they knew that almost everybody eligible to vote voted. What kind of people would want to represent you if they knew they weren't getting corporate money to do what corporate America wanted them to do? They would be compelled to do what you and I wanted them to do; you know the 200 million adults who aren't millionaires. What a concept.

One way or another there's going to be a revolution. If our citizens continue with their slothful ways and continue to be enabled by government handouts instead of understanding that a public safety net is used during the high-wire act of life and not as a bed or keep substituting a light beer for their civic duty to participate as a knowledgeable voter then the revolution will be dramatic. If, on the other hand, we have real leadership step forward to motivate the masses of people that life in America is more than an iPad or a TV remote we can avoid the ugliness of the barricades. The French tried it a few times and found it wanting as a way to reform government.

The peoples' best opportunity for this kind of change might be to demand an invocation of Article V of the Constitution. A Constitutional convention that writes a new amendment or amendments to protect the nation and its people from the corrupt influences of corporate and banking America would at least hold back the takeover by the paymasters of our elected officials on either side of the aisle and issues.

The type, style and duration of the next revolution are up to us. It's already started. Mr. Cantor's and his fellow Republicans' pugnacious and irresponsible exit from the most important bipartisan discussion going on in this country today is a clear indication of how the battle lines will be drawn.

Third World Status? It Could be U.S.

A former State Department employee, Judy Bachrach, recently wrote a piece for the *World Affairs Journal* describing her experiences in what she says was a third world nation. She qualifies a third world nation as having three particular categories:

1. A poor country with an unstable government.
2. Lacking a middle class with impoverished millions in a vast lower class.
3. A nation with a high foreign debt.

Ms. Bachrach summarizes the current state of affairs in the United States by mentioning that several foreign governments hold about $4.4 trillion in our debt. China, Hong Kong and Great Britain are some of the many countries from whom we borrow. While smaller economies like Iran and Ecuador ($13.5 billion each) also have foreign debt, it's not as large a percent of their GDPs as ours.

Regarding poverty, two years ago the United States reported having 43.6 million citizens in the "poor" category. Today, 19 million Americans live in *extreme* poverty, while the overall total of the poor has risen to almost 50 million. On the other hand, the *L.A. Times* reports the number of millionaire households in the U.S. rose by 15% in one year to 4.7 million. Larry Mishel, president of Washington-based *Economic Policy Institute* says that the recession is going to accentuate the degree of inequality in wealth. He corroborates what I and just about every other pundit have been writing for months: The middle class is shrinking, while a tiny elite of the most wealthy continue to increase its hold on domestic wealth.

The current political theater going on in our federal government plus similar political upheavals in several state governments are starting to take their toll on investors' perception of OUR governments' stability.   Who can blame them?

The U.S. House of Representatives is being held hostage by a distinct minority of 79 Tea Party advocates who have thrown one of the key elements of government stability out the window: compromise. They simply will not move off their destructive stance on the economy, the debt ceiling or the unconstitutional idea of a balanced budget amendment. Meanwhile, the House leadership continues to pander to this radical group and can't get a compromise proposal approved by the majority of House delegates (As of 7/29/2011). During all this childishness even more immaturity is exhibited by all political parties throwing brickbats back and forth. This all sounds like a dysfunctional, unstable government to me.

Hyperbole aside: No we're not a third world nation, but what sort of nation ARE we behaving like? I've written many times before that we seem to have lost our way as a great country because we no longer have a government that answers to the people. We were founded as a democratic republic, a representative democracy, yet our political process has been perverted and turned into an international laughing stock by letting massive influence in on that process by corporate/banking America. We the people have abdicated our responsibility to the few, rich moguls on Wall St. and corporate board rooms to present candidates that will do their bidding. There simply is no other explanation. The key point here is the U.S. Supreme Court's decision (*Citizens United*) of January 2010 to allow corporations and unions to contribute as much as they want to political campaigns without telling anyone. Since labor unions represent only about 13% of our workforce, even I can do the math about where the money will come from. All those infamous "think" tanks like the Cato Institute and the Heritage Foundation are funded by corporate/banking/right wing America. By giving corporations and banks "personhood", we've let the fox into our hen house, and they are eating the chickens of freedom and middle class success, while leaving the poor to their own devices.

Consider writing/calling your representatives to begin invoking Article V of the Constitution that allows us to amend it. I suggest we the people regain control of the election process by overturning the *Citizens United* decision by adding an amendment that makes all federal elections publicly funded. Add to that the elimination of the lobbying of our representatives. The middle class and the poor don't have the "equal right" to lobby because they don't have the kind of money corporate America has. Doing these two things will return the voice of government to the people, and let the rich and the corporations gain their wealth the old fashioned way: Let them EARN it.

An Embarrassment in Governing

It finally happened. Our Federal government managed to avoid destroying the country – for now. They tried mightily to ruin over 200 years of statesmanship, debate and compromise traditions and civil discourse. They failed in that task as well as the one that resulted in another stinking temporary solution to a permanent problem: Unfair distribution of wealth. How corporate/banking America got away with no change in their financial obligations to the betterment of the country can only be explained by who voted in their favor.

From a citizen's point of view, and by "citizen" I mean those of us not in the top 1%-2% of wealthy people, the bad guys won again. Worse, the newly elected members to the House of Representatives, aka, the Tea Party caucus, covered themselves with ignominy by displaying their self-serving ignorance for all to see without a whit of embarrassment. I know some Tea Party people in my community and many of them are quite embarrassed too, while others dance about as if they'd actually won something.

The winners are the rich and corporate/banking America. The losers are everybody else. There will be no deficit reduction until at least 2012 no matter what the "bill" says. We will continue to hemorrhage cash and jobs to other countries as those unaffected by the "bill" attempt to beat the coming storm of real tax and loophole reform after the next election cycle. I'm not very good at predicting things, but see if we don't end up repeating 1937.

In 1937, after almost 4 years of economic growth from the Great Depression, President Roosevelt and the Democrats lost their nerve and succumbed to the Republican pressure to reduce government spending. The result was a return to the depths of economic depression, known affectionately as the *double dip*. With job creation at a standstill, two wars on credit and no new revenues for the government plus no reduction in social services except education, I predict a second visit down this road of double-dipping. I hope I'm wrong.

I also hope we the people have finally learned our lessons: We simply have to do something about the election process. The jokes going around my e-mail world talk about how we just witnessed the second (some say third) string operating our government. Who can honestly say otherwise? The appallingly embarrassing performance of John Boehner and the House republicans covered everyone with mud of a particular type. After actually trying to exhibit statesmanship and working toward compromise with the democrats and the President, the Tea Party extremists in Congress refused to provide the votes for a balanced approach to attacking the deficit. Instead, they added a wish for a balanced budget amendment. Really? Texans have seen how well that works: They have the largest budget deficit of any state except California. Brilliant.

Feeling sorry for any republican doesn't come easy for me, but Boehner didn't deserve this from members of his own party. Then again, in a burst of political desperation, the Republican Party rushed to embrace the Tea Party to gain votes and seats in Congress.

"Be careful what you ask for" must be ringing in Boehner's ears as he tees it up back in Ohio.

While I'm at it, our President and the democrats did a pretty lousy job of standing up for their constituents. They also covered themselves with ignominy by caving in, i.e., paying the hostage takers. By allowing the republicans to attach the debt ceiling debate to the deficit reduction plans, they helped blow up the process that could have produced something that the common citizen would have seen as fair, just, intelligent and far-sighted. Instead we got this...thing.

In an article I wrote after the health care "bill" was passed, I alluded to the democrats negotiating with themselves. This time they showed how poor they are at standing by their own principles. Our politics are no longer actions of statesmanship or reason or compromise. Our politics are all about power and how it is used. In this instance the power of the presidency has been wasted and the second team in Congress committed a grievous error.

Is it any wonder that the rest of the world is embarrassed for us that we govern so badly? This is the worst performance by ANY government of mine in my lifetime.

Economic Reality: Consumers at the Brink

Yesterday, I was doing research for a book I'm co-authoring with a good friend and I began re-reading my first book, *The Voter's Guide to National Salvation,* a compendium of my published newspaper articles since December, 2009. It was spooky that so many of my predictions and summations have come true over the last few weeks. No, I'm not ready to start looking for a crystal ball on e-Bay, but it struck me as peculiar that even some amateur like me could see this mess coming from almost a year ago. This is one time when I wish it weren't so.

I listened to some pundits this morning lamenting about how automated we are such that many of our services no longer involve people, but machines and computers. Meanwhile, jobs that actually pay money are off-shored. Their point was: When do we reach the threshold where there are insufficient jobs, or jobs that pay so little that our people will NOT be able to consume? I'm sure there are charts and graphs that show when and how the individuals' earnings drop below affording anything but the very basics of life in America.

The news also informed me that at a net job creation rate of 250,000 per month, it would take 12 years to return to 2000 employment levels. Who can we thank for that? Weren't we told that tax cuts would create jobs?

Even the entertainment industry is getting hit. Golf courses are struggling nationwide, movie theaters are empty and live entertainment clubs are struggling except for the biggest draws. Have you seen the prices for seeing live entertainment? My wife and I wanted to see *Santana* next fall. At $125 each, we won't be going.

The reduction in such vaporous things as entertainment will also impact jobs. If our unemployment continues to climb, how will we be able to pay for the welfare, unemployment insurance and health care of that 20% (the real rate and climbing) who aren't working? Doesn't that mean more borrowing since we refuse to go where the money is and close tax avoidance loopholes and raise taxes on the rich? What sort of "certainty" do businesses and banks need to break loose those trillions of dollars to create jobs and provide loans for new and growing businesses as well as new homes? Why are they hoarding capital and keeping it from the consumers? As I said, if consumers have no money to consume, businesses won't be selling anything to anybody.

In this light, I have to ask what restarts economic growth: More budget cuts to government? That will just lay off more people and put them onto the welfare and unemployment rolls. Cut the military? Sure. Where will those ex-service people go for work to support their families? Cut the Pentagon budget? O.K. That means more defense industry workers hit the street. Cut welfare? Cut Medicare? Cut Medicaid? How about cutting Homeland Security? We haven't been attacked in years. How many illegal phone taps can we afford?

I ask again: What will spur economic growth? If the private sector and the banks sit on money without creating jobs or loans, who will put people to work? Am I the only one asking these questions? Do you know from where the initiative is going to arise? I've worked for several private sector businesses, both large and small. Without fail, no capital investment is made without the prospect of a market or demand from one. The initiative comes from the consumer or the potential consumer. If there is no incentive or ability to consume, there will be no market.

This is where Keynesian economics is supposed to come riding in on a silk-paper horse and prime the pump of business by offering government funded contracts to private businesses that put people to work that puts paychecks into their hands that allows them to buy homes, cars, clothes and education for their families.

Not now. No. We're all about cutting government. We're all about austerity. We're all about deficit reduction. Am I mistaken in seeing the philosophical conflict between reality of the non-working consumer and the ideals of fiscal *hawkery*?

Stop our Warring Ways!

This title sounds like a cry from the early 70s, but the fact remains that we're still fighting wars in underdeveloped countries that drain our treasury and human resources continuously. When will we ever learn? Isn't there someone somewhere that can influence our "leaders" in government to disentangle ourselves from corrupt governments and ancient cultures none of which we understand? Who gave us the "Police the World" card? Nobody. We did it on our own.

Yes, we are s-l-o-w-l-y extricating ourselves from Iraq, while the corrupt politicians we put in place still plead for more money and more American lives to risk at their behest. We've been in Iraq longer than we were in Viet Nam. Why doesn't someone in Washington and/or the pentagon just order up all the C-17s and fly everybody the heck out of there? The British evacuated an entire army from Dunkirk in 3 days in 1940. They did it with private pleasure craft as well as the navy ships they could spare. Three days!! It's still costing us around $2 billion a month in Iraq while we trickle people out of there.

On top of that, we are spending $2 billion a WEEK in Afghanistan. The original goal for invading this hostile, backward country was to defeat the Taliban and capture/kill Osama bin Laden. We helped the Afghans defeat the Taliban in pretty short order, and managed to miss bin Laden the first time at Tora Bora due to pentagon bungling. We killed bin Laden this year (2011). Mission accomplished, right? Not quite. We still have to "train" the Afghans to take care of themselves while everybody keeps trying to kill one another along the border with that other wholly trustworthy ally Pakistan. Note: These tribes have been fighting each other for about 7,000 years.

Ah, Pakistan: A nuclear power that harbored our arch enemy for 8 years. We need friends like this like we need weaker consumer confidence. Two billion dollars per week... Think what it could do here.

The national average salary for school teachers at home is about $45,000 per year. That means that one week of war could pay for almost 45,000 teachers. The average salary for an employed worker is about $42,000 per year. You get the idea. Think of it, though: a year in Afghanistan amounts to about $105 billion all of which we borrow from other countries. Do you think they'd still loan us the money if we invaded them? One hundred five billion dollars produces 2.5 million jobs. So, if we suddenly made 200,000 soldiers unemployed by quitting these two stupid wars, we'd have enough money to employ 2.3 million additional people out of the nearly 20 million who are still unemployed.

We're supposed to be a practical nation: fiscally conservative and frugal in our avoidance of waste – except when it comes to wars and the military-industrial complex. Then we become fiscally irresponsible and radically generous and wasteful. Why? Isn't it interesting that almost every state has a major military base and/or factories and businesses that support that "M-I" complex? I guess it has become political suicide to cut all that military-oriented business, so I guess we'll just keep wasting our treasure and our people because politicians just can't say no or find new ways to employ people – like with renewable energy projects.

We can now define ourselves as a country that is more geared to blowing up sand than taking care of its citizens and allowing them to enjoy the "pursuit of happiness". With all the braggadocio about "exceptionalism", I wonder why we are so reluctant to innovate and expand new industries that will serve a much nobler purpose than war.

There are at least a dozen industries in our country just waiting for the capital to employ millions. Instead we waste it on war machines and fighters in wars that have long outlived their purpose and usefulness to anyone. Some military "experts" are suggesting that we remain in Afghanistan for another 10 years. With the way things are looking in our national finance picture, those troops will certainly come home to a different country than the one they left.

The next time you contact your Congress critter, mention the numbers: $2 billion per week for 520 weeks. How many jobs will that money create? Go ahead. Ask him/her. Then dial 911.

It's Hard to be Humble

The season for candidate bashing is upon us. Does it ever stop, actually? During the last election cycle we all took our shots at the various people who had the audacity to say they wanted to represent us in government. After reading some of my own stuff during that period I hate to admit that I had Rick Perry pegged pretty well. Now that he's on the national stage – as I predicted – he is proceeding to do what he does best in Texas: invent the truth.

Perched atop that ever-present hi-boy collar is a vacant vessel of vapidity. Perry's right wing rhetoric isn't just right-ish, it's so over the top right that the Constitution must be rattling in its hermetically sealed glass case in Washington. Here comes the re-writer wannabe with spurs jangling and teeth glistening. He is said to have charisma that the other Republican candidates don't have. But that's like saying a five minute rain burst is better than our two year drought. How many science teachers have their faces in their hands wondering how their governor could say they teach creationism in their schools? All of them, that's who.

As of this writing, most Texas schools began classes for the 2011-12 school year. By the beginning of the next school year, we will have a good idea which of this stellar class of republicans will be running against the President in the 2012 election. I'll venture that just about every social studies teacher will be jumping through every hoop in the book to make the election season pertinent for their students. I hope they do, because without the interest of the electoral process imbued unto our children, we can't possibly hope they will grow up and be knowledgeable enough to actually vote their knowledge base and their conscience. The democratic republic we call the United State is in perilous times due to the lack of that interest in previous generations. My favorite bulls-eye, Perry, was "elected" by only 17% of the eligible voters in Texas because 30% aren't registered and 52% stayed home. Perry's "performance" on the national stage speaks more loudly than any pundit's pleas to pay attention for whom you vote.

One of the issues certain to arise during the election season will be foreign policy. With the rebellions throughout the Middle East we're seeing that our participation is unnecessary for the people of other countries to do their own bidding whether or not they are "friendly" to us. One way we ensure hostility toward ourselves is to put soldiers and guns on the ground in those countries.

Have you noticed that once we got out of Viet Nam that country became one of the fastest growing economies in the world? After the Vietnamese rebuilt what we spent years blowing up, they reached out and became a source of cheap labor for the endlessly searching corporations around the world. I wonder what will happen to Iraq once we finally leave the last boot print in the sand there. I'd bet that they find a way to stop killing each other for centuries old squabbles and figure out how to get their boundless oil wealth to pay for rebuilding what we tried to blow up for years.

The same, I'd bet, will happen in Afghanistan. Once we get the last C-17 off the ground filled with our troops, they'll resume their centuries old tribal wars until they realize that the rest of the world is really interested in buying their lithium (batteries), copper (electronics) and iron (everything else). Then, they'll figure out how to use all that money to rebuild the infrastructure that we tried to blow up for years.

Do you see the pattern here? I wonder which of the political stars on the right or the left will comprehend this idea that "putting boots on the ground" usually ends up costing our country billions of dollars we need for rebuilding the infrastructure that we have neglected because we are spending the money blowing up everybody else's infrastructure and making enemies everywhere.

I probably sound like an old hippie from the 60s (I am) when I write stuff like this, but then, maybe it's because I've lived long enough to see how many times we've repeated the same mistakes.

Article V

As the school year begins I am struck by the quiet anxiety I'm getting from my friends still teaching. We all are struck by the complete abandonment of our children and their teachers by what passes for government in this and most every state government controlled by republicans. The vast majority of citizens did NOT want schools and public education to be budget casualties, but that's what they got from "legislatures" and governors who are clearly beholden to something other than "We the people…"

This phenomenon of the people being abandoned by their government has been evolving for almost 30 years since the Reagan administration proclaimed that government WAS the problem. The solution to this problematic government was to cut taxes for the wealthy in a variety of ways, and de-regulate businesses and banking so the operators of corporate/banking America could do whatever they pleased. The euphemism of the day was: "To remain *competitive.*"

Well, how competitive are we now? With whom are we competing for jobs for our citizens? With whom are we competing for world class education for our children? The outcome to the lie about being competitive so corporate/banking America could de-regulate is being felt in virtually every household in the United States today. Greed has undermined every cherished ethic of sound banking and investment banking. The unfettered search for profit has sent our major corporations scurrying overseas with jobs and capital as fast as they can load the planes. With whom are they being competitive? Those corporations with foreign offices and factories are competing for which markets? Whose citizens are reaping the benefits of this industrial abdication?

People have been elected into office to do the bidding of their constituents; that's the theory. What we see instead is systematic avoidance of the peoples' desires. Nationwide polls showed that over 60% of our citizens wanted a public option for their health care coverage. More recently, over 70% of our citizens favored a balanced approach to reducing our deficits. "We the people" received none of the above from our "elected" officials. If we're a representative government, why don't our representatives listen to our desires? The answers are relatively simple.

Professional politicians are constantly running for office. Running for office at every level in this country takes lots of money. So, those candidates that are not anointed by a big money patron or corporation must become full-time fund raisers. That means they have to listen to who is paying them to run for office. Our little $25 personal checks are nice, but they don't carry much weight considering the million dollar requirements of state or national electioneering. Guess who the candidate listens to most.

In January, 2010, the U.S. Supreme Court ruled in the *Citizens United v. Federal Election Committee* case that corporations and unions could contribute unlimited sums of money to any candidate or campaign they wanted because they were given the status of being people. How a piece of paper from a state government certifying a corporation becomes a person is beyond my knowledge of biology and reason. This ruling effectively takes the common citizen out of the game for either running for office or having anything to say about who DOES run for office. The name of our country should now be the *United States of Big Money America.*

There is recourse to this plutocratic takeover of our country. Article V of the Constitution says that Congress, or state legislatures can call for a convention to amend the Constitution if two-thirds of either vote to do so. Then, the amendment must be passed by three-fourths of the states. In order to break the back of the corporate takeover of our country, why don't we demand that all electioneering and elections be publicly funded with a stringent petition process necessary to get their names on ballots? Furthermore, wouldn't it be interesting to see what sort of laws evolved if lobbying, either directly or indirectly, of a publicly elected official was made illegal?

You can see the difficulty here trying to get professional politicians to vote for something that effectively makes their jobs harder to retain. We the people have a lot of work to do if we intend to save our country from the internal assaults from plutocrats and oligarchs.

No End to Outrage

We've seen outrageous performances in disinformation, partisan bickering, and outright character assassination extending from the 2008 presidential campaign to the present. Some of the stuff we see, hear and read is astounding in its imagination, depths of depravity and abject cynicism.

A few highlights (lowlights) of this, our season of most serious discontent, begin with Sen. Paul Ryan's (R-WI) plan to "end Medicare as we know it." What he really meant to say, after reading the details, is that Medicare will end and we will use vouchers to pay for our health care via his good friends in the medical insurance industry. While the rest of the world enjoys significantly healthier people due, in major part, to a single-payer, universal, government sponsored health care program, we flounder in the swamp of for-profit health care.

The Republican Party campaigned mightily on a "jobs, jobs, jobs" mantra that too many people believed in 2010. Additionally, the party embraced the fledgling Tea Party movement because they were desperate for votes from the radical fringe of American politics (?). So far, not a single jobs bill sponsored by any republican in either house of Congress has been forthcoming. Instead, we get screaming partisanship about debt ceilings and balanced budgets. All this continues while corporations get virtually interest free money from banks that were saved by TARP. Few jobs become available, however, because of market "uncertainty". So, trillions of dollars sit idle while unemployed workers watch their representatives go about cutting their support systems while ensuring that the rich retain their tax favorability.

The two paragons of vacuousness, Michele Bachmann and Rick Perry tell us that 47% of Americans pay no taxes and that the tax base should be broadened to include these deadbeats. What they don't tell you is that 90% of those not paying taxes earn less than $40,000 per year and are currently exempt while corporations like G.E., eBay, Verizon and Exxon-Mobil pay *no* taxes or get refunds. The other 10% pay no taxes because their accountants and lawyers (they can afford them) find ways to avoid paying them. How can anyone still able to sip tea not see what is going on?

Hurricane Irene tattooed the Eastern seaboard with serious wind and water damage. Eric Cantor, the U.S. representative from Virginia whose district also experienced a significant earthquake said something remarkably inane by suggesting that disaster assistance should be paid for by cuts to other programs. Where has this guy been the last 235 years? We have always, *always* aided *other* countries that experienced natural disasters without hesitation and without question. Cantor thinks aid to Americans injured and made homeless by natural events should be a fiscal issue instead of a humanitarian one.

It gets worse.

A widely read right wing blog has recently published an article about helping poorer Americans register to vote then helping them to get to the polls. This article assumes that these new, poor voters will immediately try to vote for more free handouts from the government because of what and who they are. Worse, this piece goes on to accuse the President (again) of being complicit with this scheme that they thought up. They say helping the poor to vote or get registered to vote is un-American because it promotes the welfare state agenda. Now, *that* takes some gall to attack voters' rights because they *might* vote for more welfare. Unbelievable!

Many of my friends and acquaintances from both sides of the political spectrum are outraged at these vicious displays of hubris, selfishness and outright hostility to those less fortunate. Personally, I am disgusted and appalled that things have come this far.

It's bad enough that Dick Cheney has to keep trying to take credit for catching and killing bin Laden, while accusing the current President of being "ineffective" irrespective of the 18 month job growth in our stumbling economy. While facing outright Republican obstructionism, this administration has managed to retain dignity and move the country forward, whereas the opponents have lost not only their dignity, but their credibility as well.

There can be no end to outrage at these things from people who actually care about others, are true to their faith and are proud to help their fellow American. Some of us are still getting over our outrage from the previous administration's debacle. Now we have to endure more of it with this batch of republicans.

We the People are the Government

The first few words of the preamble to the Constitution say it's so. It is us who enable those WE select to represent us in the government WE are supposed to create. This defines the *democratic republic* that our founding fathers devised so painfully and carefully. In 222 years only 27 amendments have been made to this document. It used to be that Americans revered the Constitution, understood the peoples' role in governing and went about selecting *real* people to represent them.

Somewhere along the way government became the villain. In a perverse twist, Ronald Reagan said that government WAS the problem. Really? Did he mean that the very document he pledged on the Bible to defend was mistaken about government of, by and for the people? Was he right, or did he mean that it was what government *became* that was the problem? This mantra about big government being the bad guy has become the mainstream rant for conservatives, republicans and tea baggers.

Paul Begala, a historical scholar says, "The U.S. federal government is the greatest force for good in human history." I agree. Those who rail against government with the caveat about its size and how it spends money fail to say how large it should be and how much it should spend. Anybody who can identify and support those two premises should be published in all media immediately. The most spectacular successes of any country in human history belong to us: *We the people* of the United States of America.

We can take credit for those successes because we resisted the charlatans who tried to make our labor force into serfs for their lordships, among other things. We overcame ingrained prejudice to bring women and people of color into our sphere of governing and participating in that government. Nobody has done it better than we have....we the people.

Right wing extremism has hijacked the Republican Party to the extent that our government is not responding to the desires of the people it is supposed to represent. In fact, the influence of corporate money on both major political parties has diminished the voice of the people to a mere whisper. These extremists, aka, the Tea Party are the new charlatans. They rave on about fiscal responsibility and the Constitution's controls on spending, yet fail to understand what the phrase "promote the general welfare" means. To these people the only welfare that concerns them is their own. This was evidenced recently on a TP sponsored "debate" where destitute people needing medical care were jeered. These are the same people who insist that this nation was founded on Christian principles. It wasn't, but the stupefying hypocrisy of the TP is most evident.

Here are some examples of what the people are NOT getting from their government even though they petition it to do so.

- Over 60% wanted a public option (Medicare) for their health care.
- Over 70% want a balanced approach to reduce the deficit.
- Over 60% wanted stricter gun control laws.
- Over 60% didn't want public education cuts.

More people now believe (78%) that their representatives no longer represent their interests. Sixty-three percent think that small business owners are more capable of solving our problems than the professional politicians "elected" to office. The people are calling for a stop to the wars draining our treasury. They are calling for improved schools and an elimination of extensive testing. They are asking for new revenue to be raised by taxing gambling, marijuana, tobacco, luxury autos and even prostitution. Ninety-one percent of us say our elected representatives fail to address the nation's problems. (*Newsweek, 9/19/2011*)

We the people must step up and retake our government from "we the corporation". The professional politicians must be replaced by citizens beholden to only their constituents and not lobbyists or big money interests.

WE are the people and it is OUR government, not the professionals' who represent only the rich and the powerful. It is up to us to overthrow the yoke of oppression from those in the ivory towers. Ask yourself, "If not now, when? If I don't become active, then who will?" It's up to us. We haven't a day to lose.

Spinning Away Toward Oblivion

Things must be getting desperate for the republican caucus in Washington and state capitols around the country. While the republican "leadership" keeps stomping their Gucci clad feet against anything the President or the democratic caucus presents as plans or ideas to solve the jobs crisis, the deficit "crisis" and the foreign policy crises, the people are waking up to the facts and realities all sentient (intelligent) citizens have: We need to get back to work as a nation. Unemployed people pay NO taxes, thus reducing revenue even more so than the rich who have "lawyered" their way out of paying them. Our once world class manufacturing base is all but gone. We are losing the ability, as a nation, to put people to work.

President Obama's jobs plan receives a 45% approval from the people while only 32% say otherwise. I guess the other 13% don't care. Regarding the people's opinions on who should be paying more taxes, the numbers are truly startling, even for a jaded progressive. Eighty percent of *moderates* want the rich to pay more taxes and have loopholes closed for corporations. Sixty-eight percent of *independents* feel the same way. The big surprise: Fifty one percent of REPUBLICANS think the rich should pay more taxes. Maybe those republicans, who are not as wealthy as they'd like to be, or who have seen that their dream of becoming rich is not going to happen anytime soon, are coming to their senses. Maybe they have begun to see that we are INDEED all in this together and that the *cuts only* mantra of the Tea Party and other extremists is NOT the way to row this boat.

Meanwhile we have the spinners in Congress saying really nasty, disrespectful things about our working class families. John Boehner, the Speaker of the House and third in the line of succession to be President said that providing more unemployment compensation for the long-term unemployed was like giving more cocaine to a cocaine addict. Wow! How's that for respect? I wonder how those hard working families feel about being lumped in with criminals and sloths.

Boehner's accusation about Obama's plan to reduce the deficit as "class warfare" is ludicrous. Have you noticed that it's only class warfare when the rich are asked to pay their fair share? This is nothing new. The rich screamed bloody murder when FDR raised their taxes to help pay for that little disturbance on opposite sides of the world, aka World War II. Do you think the poor, the chronic underclass and the downward spiraling middle classes (i.e., the vast majority) are saying that it is class warfare for everyone to pay their fair share?

In the strictest sense, it has always been about class warfare. After the Civil War, carpetbaggers went south and tried to get rich off the chaos there. The Robber Barons went to work as the industrial revolution kicked into high gear squeezing every dime they could from the working classes to enrich themselves. They sneered at the "rabble" of the working people. The ivory tower boys are still trying to get rid of unions, because "they" are the problem with competitiveness. Maybe that's why corporate America continues to sit on $2 trillion instead of creating jobs. Class warfare....

By the way, history shows us that most businesses that become unionized deserve it. Most Americans are "rugged individualists" and don't really want to bond together except when they have to. When working conditions are dangerous, degrading, unhealthy and clearly exploitive, an organized work force is the next, certain outcome.

Putting spin on the growing economic inequities in this country by demonizing "redistribution of wealth" as if it were the vortex to hell is simply irresponsible demagoguery of the worst kind. It isn't socialism when the government provides a safety net for those less fortunate, especially when those most fortunate have caused the problem in the first place. It isn't socialism to have single payer, government sponsored health care – like the rest of the civilized world – especially when we rank in the 30s in health quality. It isn't socialism to have public assistance programs that help people develop skills and abilities so they can work and support their families.

The spinners seem to think that everything about the idea of socialism is evil when in fact our society operates – and must operate – with many, many socialistic agencies. They missed the point about what made and makes our nation great. It's called taking care of one another and showing initiative instead of greed. Otherwise, oblivion is our final rotation from this right wing spin.

What Hath Reagan Wrought?

From some of the lies, disinformation, demagoguery and pure scatological nonsense coming from the current field of republican presidential candidates, I am more convinced than ever that the Reagan era began the slow but decided turn to the political right by our country. What would Ronnie have thought of a candidate who first plagiarized the arch disinformation dispenser, Rush Limbaugh, then repeated the lie of no jobs from the 2009 stimulus by the utterly classless framing of it using a neighbor's dog, and shovel ready jobs? I'd guess that he would be utterly ashamed.

He would also be utterly ashamed at the nakedness of crony capitalism practiced by the leading candidate – if you believe polls these days. Reagan would be cringing at the mindless babbling of Santorum, Bachmann, Perry, Cain, Gingrich and Paul who have yet to identify a cogent reason for them becoming President. Poor Jon Huntsman… He's the only republican making any sense, talking about real issues that need solutions and maintaining an above the slime personage along the way. Sadly, he's running far behind the stylized, self-made professional candidates, Romney, Gingrich, Cain and Perry, thus removing any intelligence from the campaign. He's the only candidate who seems to be made out of something sterner than sound bites and gotcha lines. He will, of course, never be nominated to represent THIS Republican Party next November. Poor Ronnie: What have you wrought?

Well, for one thing you, Mr. President, bought into Wall St. and Milton Friedman big time. Supply-side economics became the be all and end all to all things conservative – or so you thought. Too bad it doesn't work in the real world. You were talked into hiring Donald Regan out from under his mantel of lordliness at Merrill-Lynch. You let the Republican Congress that rode your long coattails start deregulating business and banking. You attacked labor unions as the bad guys preventing your pals on Wall St. from taking it all. The foxes saw the gate to the hen house had opened and rushed in to carve up the great money pot pie known as the United States of America. While corporate/banking America was munching away on populace chicken you were telling the chickens still living how bad government was. Well, you now have your self-fulfilling prophecy coming true.

Our government is a problem, a big problem. It's still there, but it has become a lead weight on the psyche and confidence of the American people. It has been bloated to more than double its size since you were President. This government has also abandoned the people as it never did before. By allowing corporations to drive the election process – as they have for the decades since you left office – the candidate quality has declined precipitously. We are presented with professional politicians instead of statesmen and women. Their only purpose is to get elected and reelected to stay in power. This is evidenced most dramatically by the current slate of republicans running for President. Furthermore, the "professionals" in both houses of Congress are a pitiful representation of the dignity of the American people. Their mindless squabbling over issues while completely ignoring the desires and needs of their constituents is the lowest of low points in our government's history.

Additionally, "trickle-down", get-government-out-of-the-way politics has created an enabled class of businessmen who whine about being taxed even after they've been allowed to hide money in foreign banks, are subsidized by taxpayer handouts so they can pay their stockholders, and continue to hoard capital while thumbing their collective noses at the American worker. We have the richest in America screaming about the taxes they don't pay even though when they do pay some, they pay less than the working men and women who sweat for *their* wealth.

Government is now so frightened about suggesting things that we used to do for greatness (major highways, dams, space exploration, economic expansions, mass transport) that we do nothing to define ourselves while cutting valuable infrastructure like educating our children.

The short-term profit mentality has one major problem. When people/consumers have no money to consume because their jobs left the country with no replacement job, how do capitalists expect to obtain more capital? How do industrialists expect to make and sell more products when the marketplace is barren? How do families support themselves when they can't afford food and health care?

What do we do now, Ronnie?

The Will and the Way

Some preliminary work has been done with developing and implementing an "intelligent" grid network of electrical energy supply to every home, shop, mine, factory and school in America. This concept is intended to replace the hodgepodge of state and local networks that are connected to one another in a wide variety of ways. The problem is that efficiency is low and the service security is at high risk while we continue to expand national electrical needs. Visionaries and engineers see a common, integrated electrical grid system from the point of generation to the energy efficient bulb in your bedside lamp.

Some also see our current grid as vulnerable to security from terrorists, anarchists or other disruptive forces that would bring our nation to a screeching halt if key interruptions occurred at critical places and times. Since there is no coherent system of redundancy that would make up for local grid failures, a rolling shutdown is likely to result. Obviously, this is no small project, and that's where the problem with implementing an intelligent grid network becomes most difficult.

A recent MSNBC blurb featuring Rachel Maddow triggered this piece when she stood before Hoover Dam and said that an entire nation was required to produce such a successful project. The Hoover Dam project was completed in the mid-1930s when our country was in the midst of a deep economic depression. Today, even as its innermost concrete is still curing, this dam supplies the entire southwestern United States with reliable electricity produced by falling water. How did this happen?

It happened because WE decided it would happen and went and built it. That was the "will" to do great things. Our government, strapped for cash at the time, borrowed money and funded the project for hundreds of private contractors. The United States government does not own and operate a dam building entity. The Hoover Dam project employed thousands of men and women for several years of work who would have otherwise been unemployed and on the government dole. We gathered our best resources and put them to work. That was the "way" we did it.

Projects like Hoover Dam exemplify American greatness – when we were great and exceptional. The intelligent grid idea is as necessary today as Hoover Dam was back in the middle of the last century. Questions like "Do we have the technology and know-how to do this." The answer is, "Yes." The technology is not that sophisticated. New links between power sources that are adjusted to a standardized quality and operated by modern computers is almost off-the-shelf. So, what are we waiting for?

Our current political and social situation shows that we lack the will to do great things. Short term profiteering, one of the worst political environments in our history and a fundamental lack of visionary leadership all contribute to our inability to do exceptional things. Instead of putting people to work on infrastructure projects like intelligent grid, we sell fighter planes to Iraq. Instead of analyzing how we spend our money on educating our children, we cut the funding so we can balance budgets without asking the wealthiest and the profiteers to pay their fair share of revenues. In short, we have lost our ability to be great. We have willfully given in to the god of profit at the expense of those things that made us the greatest nation on Earth.

The corruption that corporate/banking America has fostered in government and foisted on the American people while sitting on trillions of dollars of un-committed capital continues to cloud any vision for doing what is right for the working people in this country. While the two major political parties hurl brickbats at one another and act like spoiled children, our children go wanting for knowledge. While so-called political party leaders commit all their energy to ousting a President, our nation's infrastructure crumbles.

Will private, free market enterprise come to the rescue of political gridlock and execute necessary projects like the intelligent grid, or will the hoarding of capital and divisiveness of our citizenry be the watchword for the next 20 years? Who will understand that educating our children as the rest of the world does will at least put us back to the level of first world nations?

Life in Boehnerville

Life is different in Boehnerville. It's much simpler there. There, job-*creators* get all the rewards, but job-*performers*, not so much. There, *opportunity* is everything; *acting on opportunity,* no meaning. In Boehnerville, a stage full of musical instruments, *but no musicians* suffices for a symphony orchestra. In Boehnerville, a fine collection of recipes exists, *but with no chef* it suffices as a Five-Star restaurant. There, an array of neighborhood schools exists, *but with no teachers.* This suffices for a K-12 educational system. There, a fine assortment of fire-fighting equipment, *but no firemen* suffices for a fire department. There, a state-of-the-art hospital, *but no doctors and nurses* suffices for adequate medical care.

Yes, indeed, life is really much simpler in Boehnerville, but if we continue to listen to certain political voices, we can bring life, as *it is in Boehnerville,* to Anywhere, U.S.A: life where *employers* get all the rewards for jobs *created* and *employees* few of the rewards for jobs *performed if they're asked to perform at all!*

The above idea and some examples are credited to a friend and colleague. We have contended for some time that the fraud being foisted on the American people by the reckless and anti-citizen (never mind the middle class) policies of this Congress is a result of the duality that operates both major parties. On the one hand you have the super rich, big business and banking who buy as many politicians as they can. On the other hand you have the Tea Party that keeps pounding the empty drum of their ignorance and hate for anything and everything they don't understand as they scare the mainstream Republicans.

The question, "Where were the deficit hawks when the Bush II administrations eschewed all pretense about fair and balanced economics and went hell-bent into colossal debt?" has been asked hundreds of times with almost the same number of answers. The most obvious answer grouping centers on the lack of real leadership in the Republican caucus. Similar to the Democrat's problems with coherent policy and leadership, the Republicans have succumbed to perhaps the most scurrilous faction since the "plug uglies" before the Civil War.

Boehner was on the brink of a deal with the President when Eric Cantor, the Tea Party caddy, intimidated the process such that Ohio John was left using such catchy phrases as "negotiating with this White House is like trying to pin Jell-O to a wall". Or, something equally inane about moving goal posts. Irrespective of Boehner's poetic challenges, the point is he lets the Tea Party wag his dog. The cynical view of this situation clearly favors those who are "quietly" taking our capital and our jobs to the far reaches of the planet and leaving the middle classes scuffling for the leftovers. This is all in the name of fiscal "restraint", mind you.

Recent college graduates have never had this much trouble finding a professional job associated with their degree since the Great Depression. The middle classes have not had this much trouble making ends meet or been at this level of food and shelter insecurity since the Great Depression. NEVER before has the economic gap between the rich and everybody else been this wide. While that gap continues to grow, research shows that it began to increase rapidly in size about the time the Bush II tax cuts helped destroy fiscal responsibility. The gap grew as Wall St. and the banks were deregulated allowing the greed merchants to vastly increase investor wealth while selling bad loans a few times and collecting on the margins. The gap grew when the Bush II administration violated one of its own talking points about competition and gave the drug companies guaranteed profits for not only themselves but the health care insurance companies as well.

These policies coupled with the lethargy and ignorance of the electorate allowed the building of Boehnerville to proceed apace. Well, take a good look. The ivory towers in the middle of town belong to John's country club pals. The crumbling hovels interspersed between collapsed bridges, pot-holed roads and decrepit schools belong to what used to be the middle class. The tarpaper shacks and the refrigerator cartons are where the poor live, just as they always have. Welcome to the future in Boehnerville.

The Next Bubble

Remember when Ross Perot made that famous comment about that "giant sucking sound..."? He was talking about American jobs heading south of the border. His prediction was a little early, but he was right. Corporate America, encouraged and rewarded by NAFTA, has sent over 6 million good paying jobs to Mexico, Asia and Europe. This is their gift to the American worker so they can be more "competitive".

Those of us who read things other than our iPads have seen the graphs that show how the distribution of wealth has skyrocketed toward the top over the last 20-30 years. We've seen how American CEOs now earn 10 times more than their European counterparts and keep trying to increase that margin. Why? They do it because they are compelled to do it. That is pure capitalism at work. Competition in business is doing whatever it takes to outdo the other guy competing for market share. Without regulation by government, this basic operating system becomes a vicious, cruel and inhuman practice. Our own industrial history is full of evidence that supports that statement.

There is much complaining from the "conservatives" about overburdening regulation of business. Maybe they're right, but there are reasons for those regulations. Most of them exist to protect PEOPLE from being abused, exploited, placed in danger or unfairly treated all in the name of profit. The other regulations not directly used to protect people are used to protect the environments in which they live. Pure capitalism, you see, is not people friendly. Its only philosophy is: If something increases profits it is good. From Gordon Gecko in the first *Wall Street* movie: "Greed is good!"

When the housing and loan bubble burst, even the banks admitted that they let greed run amok. How was this allowed to happen? The banks/Wall St. spent the last 30 years trying to get deregulated so they could do just what they did. The few who were in on the ground floor literally made billions while the working classes lost their homes, jobs and health care. The next bubble, poverty, is now growing as a result.

How well do we understand poverty? I've seen it, but haven't lived it. I've known people who are very poor and I know some who have worked their way out of it. Those who escaped poverty in the U.S. had help. Yes, they put forth the majority of the effort, but somebody or something threw them a rope from which they could pull themselves up.

Government statistics today tell us that 15% of our population lives in poverty. Those 47-50 million people receive new members every day as the middle class continue to lose their jobs, homes and wealth. The downward spiraling middle class is entering the poverty vortex. The only social group not experiencing economic decay is the wealthy. The gap between the wealthy and the poor continues to grow. That fuels the bubble's growth.

The seemingly disorganized movement around the nation that began with the Occupy Wall Street demonstrations is the public display of that bubble. Not all the demonstrators are poor or unemployed, but the vast majority is. They have stories that tell how their hopes and dreams have been destroyed by the economic failures of the last 10 years brought about by greed. All the major capitalistic countries in the world share culpability in this great unregulated grab for unseemly wealth, and we now see how vulnerable the global economy is to a few irresponsible merchants of that greed.

I recently learned that the words "poverty" or "the poor" were never mentioned in the presidential debates in 2008 by any of the candidates. So, who is the voice of the poor in this country? Why aren't those who claim to be such good Christians not heeding His words from the Book of Matthew? Jesus attempted to look after the poor; he was their champion. Are any of today's politicians talking about the poor and poverty? I haven't heard anyone speak of the poor. So, who among them, who keep telling us how we are founded on Christian principles, is going to step up and shed the mantle of hypocrisy before the poverty bubble bursts?

Adding it Up

Have you ever noticed how many people and groups republicans say they don't like or are against in some way? If you listen to the auricle of self, Eric Cantor, you hear the word "mob" used to describe the "Occupy" groups around the country. What did he call the Tea Party rallies before last November's election? Well organized, peaceful demonstrations. I guess he missed the part where some of those "peaceful" demonstrators brought loaded M-16 assault rifles to them.

The "mob" represents a wide cross-section of America that is unemployed, under-employed, bankrupt, foreclosed, under water on mortgages and college loans, gay, liberal, progressive, union members, teachers, retired military veterans and skilled trade people displaced by exported jobs. Yes, some of these categories overlap, but it does beg the question: Who is left? Who does the GOP like?

Well, they've got those backwards thinking tea partiers. Then there are the 400 top rich people who own more wealth than any other 50% of Americans you can put together. Who can forget those banking executives and their caddy, Tim Geithner, the guy they got into the Obama administration as Secretary of the Treasury? Certainly the corporate leaders of America are part of the GOP "base" of appreciators. These are the guys sitting, collectively, on $4 trillion of capital that is not doing anything except earning more interest for the banks and the corporations. Jobs? What jobs?

When I see the signs on TV or the paper that say, "We are the 99%" I understand better what they mean. What is left for the GOP to like is the 1% that sends them all that money for them to get re-elected. Now, I'm not so narrow-minded that I assume that that 1% aren't hedging (pun intended) their bets by not funding democrats too. After all, over half the Senate and the President are democrats.

What the 99% are beginning to act upon is that 1% that owns and operates the government and is not serving their interests. Wall Street is merely the symbolic gathering place for protest against the big money interests running the show. Meanwhile, the 99% are left with barely enough to live on, (never mind aspiring to improved lifestyle) whether they're willing to work hard, or not. To them, it doesn't seem to matter. Most the money is locked up with the top 1%. In fact 80% of all the money is held by that 1%. The top 5% own over 90% of the money and wealth. This doesn't add up to a happy scenario for the 90%-99% who are left to scramble for the rest.

This situation has been festering for a long time. Working people have generally kept their heads down and tried to improve their lot within the existing system. But after bank deregulation, unfair (to American workers) trade agreements, union busting and extensive tax loophole exploitation there was little left for the majority of our citizens to work for. They began to realize that they were becoming the serfs of yore. What is equally amazing is that many who vote strictly and repeatedly republican are in this group of scramblers too. That is certainly their choice, but one might ask why they'd keep voting against their own interests.

The current demonstrations around the world signify that the people have had enough of the current situation. They want to take their country back from the money changers in the temples of greed in New York and around the world. They are demanding a fair share. We've heard this before.

The right wing media and politicians will demonize the demonstrators and trivialize the demonstrations. They do so at their own peril. This movement isn't going away until the guaranteed rights to have grievances redressed are enacted.

The demonstrations in the "occupy" movements are conducted peacefully right now. The people in them can add up their chances of living the American dream and appreciating the social promises made them from previous generations of citizens demonstrating that their voices be heard by their representatives. They are trying to heal the rending of the social fabric made by republican intransigence and favoritism toward the wealthy. In the end, they will be responsible for sweeping the Republican Party hacks out of office next November.

The Land of the Free

Someone sent me a disturbing video clip wherein some British commentators were discussing our prisons and, more accurately, the numbers of American citizens in them compared to the rest of the world. Here is the site where you can share my astonishment: http://www.youtube.com/watch?v=nPZed8af9RI&feature=share

When I taught school in Colorado, some family friends conducted religious services for prisoners in the state prison system. They sent me some chilling statistics that, for the first time in my life, made me realize how pervasive incarceration in our country really is. I learned that 75% of those in jail are functionally illiterate and it cost the state more to house a prisoner for a year than the starting salary of a school teacher. That correlation was more than a little ironic to me. The year was 1995. Since then the numbers have become increasingly unfavorable to validating our prison system.

The questions keep coming: What are we doing with these people? Are we rehabilitating them, or warehousing them? Why are 75% of the inmates in for non-violent crimes like drug possession, sales and distribution of drugs? Then: Why are we spending countless billions on "drug wars" when the usage and arrests keep climbing? Are we allowing this to support the private enterprise prison business? Is this what we have become as a nation?

It is now common knowledge that we, "the land of the free", incarcerate more people than any other nation on Earth. That is NOT per capita. We warehouse 2.3 million people for mostly non-violent crimes, with more on the way. What are our answers from government and politicians? "Build more prisons!" In conjunction with that last statement it should be noted that prisons are increasingly being operated by private contractors instead of state agencies. There have been several corruption scandals regarding kickbacks to judges and prosecutors making sure those "private enterprises" remain profitable.

Of course we all want to be safe from criminals, so let's look at what criminals are doing. If the 75% drug-related crimes are accurate, and that our law enforcement people tell us they catch only 50% of the potential drug crime people, that must mean that something like 6-10% of our citizens are illegally using, growing, selling and making illegal drugs. Why is this happening in our wonderful country? Don't all our citizens find the United States the best place on Earth to live? What's wrong with them? Why do they need to escape the realities of their lives?

If these crimes were restricted to those who law enforcement or most upstanding citizens called "low lifes", maybe we could accept this. Increasingly, though, the people with lots of money are buying and using the drugs. I'm sure the actor Michael Douglas can tell you all about his son's adventures to corroborate that fact.

While taking care to not make false correlations between different data, I can't help but note that most of the children who drop out of school do so because of lack of interest. These data are coincident with the advent of extensive testing associated with *No Child Left Behind*. Having taught school in this environment I can say first hand that utilizing watered down curricula and still keeping kids interested was my biggest challenge. So, I supplemented weak parts of the curriculum and expanded the information and lesson designs that DID keep children interested and motivated.

What I'm suggesting is that we have a serious systemic problem with our way of life. Chipping away at symptoms like building more prisons for an obviously flawed legal system and myopic government policies will never get to the cause of the problem. We may not be asking the right questions or listening to the answers from our people.

Of course there will always be the experimenters and those who tempt forbidden fruits. That is normal. But the pandemic use of very harmful drugs by our children and adults goes beyond causal experimentation.

Poverty is the driving force behind most crime. People in poor neighborhoods get the weakest public education. Poor people also have the poorest nutrition, the lowest opportunity for quality parenting and the highest frequency of violent crime. We know that just throwing money at the problem without oversight won't cure the systemic problem.

Perhaps providing opportunities to train poor people with the skills to build their own lives as a first priority is the answer. The 15% of the people in poverty who supply 90% of our incarcerated citizens must not think they are very free.

The CCC means "Yes, Yes, Yes"

I just watched a recently made documentary about the Civilian Conservation Corps. The similarities between the terribly tough times of the 1930s and today's sagging national infrastructure were significant enough for me to think of ways this program could benefit today's situation.

The inception of the CCC went from FDR's desk to putting people on the trains to work camps in less than 3 months. The Congress, desperate to do anything to put people to work funded it. The CCC collected young men in their teens and early 20s who were poor, hopeless and, in some cases, illiterate and signed them up for a dollar a day wages. Twenty-five of the $30 per month was to be sent home to their families. In 2011 dollars that would be equivalent to about $30 per day or $900 per month, $750 of which would go home. The volunteers were housed, clothed, fed and allowed into town once per week.

At its peak, the CCC employed over 2 million young men who worked less than 8 hours per day, but built national infrastructure that lasts to this day and that we who have visited national and state parks enjoy still. There were over 80 such camps in Texas alone. The ripple effect of this program was not just limited to the young men who built all the things we enjoy, but it also employed cooks, teachers for the illiterate, engineers, surveyors, truck drivers, expert tradesmen to train in construction skills, nurses, doctors and a variety of other "regular" employees. The materials for building and the food for feeding the camps spurred those businesses that provided these goods by infusing much needed cash. That cash was subsequently spent on hiring more labor at the work sites of the suppliers who, in turn, spent their pay on groceries, cars, cloths and education. When money circulates economies boom.

We face today an equally sluggish economy caused, coincidentally, by many of the same foibles of unregulated banking we had in the 1920s and revived in 1980 that pushed the entire world's economy to the brink of collapse in 2008. We have a crumbling physical infrastructure like bridges, roads, schools, government buildings and housing...the list goes on. We have an increasingly uneducated populace with 40% of our children dropping out and not receiving a high school diploma. Seventy-five percent of our incarcerated people are functionally illiterate. Teachers' jobs and libraries are being cut for short-sighted deficit reduction while we continue to spend $2.5 billion per day on "defense". The time seems right for another try at something like the CCC in 2012.

If we paid our unemployed minimum wage for a standard work month of about 200 hours, we're adding $1500 per month to their lives which is more than most unemployment programs. If these workers send the majority of this money home to their families or even to their own savings account, the cash will reenter circulation instead of sitting in some computer or vault. Yes, it will cost money to feed and house the workforce, but we've done that before and know how to do it inexpensively. In the 1930s, the Army ran the camps. With all the food we throw away, much of it could be utilized for this project. Meanwhile, our infrastructure repair would proceed at least to a point where private specialty companies could pick up and complete them.

Unemployed teachers and craftsmen and women could be hired to teach and train a whole new generation of workers such that upon their completion of the new CCC enlistment they could return to their hometowns and be available to apply their skills and experience in private sector jobs. We might not hear any more stories about welding companies not being able to find skilled workers for their projects like we do today. Since our public schools have dropped most heavy vocational programs for austerity, the degradation of our skilled labor force has sunk to dangerous levels.

The new CCC would re-energize our workforce, build new skill bases and give our otherwise underemployed, bored and counterproductive citizens a chance to earn a living instead of expecting to be handed one. I'd say "YES" to this in a minute.

Getting Lucky

It's hard for me to admit it, but I may have been wrong about slamming the Bush II administration so hard. I may also have been wrong about giving Ronald Reagan such a rough ride. Perhaps having Grover Norquist act like an ideological geek isn't such a bad thing, pledges and all. In fact, I'm beginning to think that having these people, along with their pals Karl Rove, Dick Cheney, Dick Armey, Tom DeLay, Roger Ailes, Lee Atwater, Paul Wolfowitz and the gabbling neo-conservatives enter our history when they did is the best thing that could have happened to the United States.

The "Occupy" movements made me think about why these folks are demonstrating. Are they just upset with the 1% of the super rich who own more than 50% of the country's wealth, or are they just frustrated that their college degrees, military service, skilled craftsmanship and artistic talents can't earn them more than a meager existence, the one they hoped to avoid with hard work, diligence and continued education? Maybe they've read and seen enough of the injustice, hopelessness, crumbling infrastructure, declining public services and education and condescension the working classes have to endure in an ever increasing elitist-controlled society. Maybe it's the sadness associated with having the moral and societal pact torn up between the working people in America and those who control the money that creates jobs. Maybe it's all of these things....and more.

Maybe the demonstrators are out there because of guilt. Maybe they're embarrassed for having ignored the growing corruption and graft that has put us in this pickle. After decades of poor voter turnout, a 24/7/365 election cycle that drains millions of dollars from productive endeavors , bought and paid for politicians, a complicit Supreme Court that has an elitist, ruling class agenda, industrial and capitalistic moguls who eagerly send our jobs to other countries then hide their assets so they can avoid taxes and a "let 'em eat cake" attitude from their "elected" representatives, they are compelled to demand what their government promised but did not deliver: CHANGE.

The fat, dumb and happy society finally saw what was happening from 30 years of creeping elitism and unregulated capitalism. They had to be shocked and insulted into realizing that they were lied to and manipulated by those they trusted with their country. These people out in the rain, the cold, the tear gas, the rubber bullets and the nightsticks now want to vent their anger AND their guilt. They didn't take charge of their country because they thought that a representative government would take care of them, protect them from the greed of the money interests and produce legislation that was good for their pursuit of happiness. They were wrong. They now know they let it happen. "We the People...." didn't do our jobs.

So, what are our jobs? If the current situation is any guide, maybe we should promote voter sophistication as a major household activity. Maybe we should all educate ourselves to the laws that affect us, examine the veracity of the people who say they want to represent us, study the issues put on the ballot and become active in putting things on the ballot that are good for the people and our communities. Maybe we should insist that everyone in our families and neighborhoods be registered to vote and also aware of who and what is on the ballot. This is hard to do, but so are the alternatives of having no home, no money, no health care and no honest representation.

Those demonstrators occupying this or that city must realize what they are doing and why they are doing it. If they don't they'll be just like the uninformed voters who put the people in office (against which they are demonstrating) that caused this mess in the first place. I'd love to see some signs that say: "We must have 100% voter turnout!"

Yes, we got lucky. Just in time, too. If the people had waited much longer, perhaps ALL their opportunities, jobs and dreams would end up in Malaya, India, China or Europe. Thank goodness those I mentioned earlier here were so disruptive to American life that it woke up the people.

Where are We Headed?

Believe it or not, I read conservative columns and gain insight and balance as a result. I avoid certain right wing ideologues because they, like so many pundits on the left, spout company line after company line. It gets boring and predictable. There are a few writers like Friedman, Pitts and Dowd that are insightful, intelligent and entertaining. My favorite conservative writer is David Brooks, and this week he wrote a column that caught my attention.

Brooks discussed the long-held dream of most Americans, upward mobility. He mentions two kinds of inequality: BLUE inequality, the type separating the higher salary earners and everybody else in and around big cities. RED inequality is that gap between college graduates and everybody else in smaller towns and cities. In "blue" areas, 69% of the top 1% earners operate some sort of financial business. The other 31% are the doctors, lawyers, athletes and engineers. You'll notice that there is no mention of manufacturing industry here.

In 1979, Brooks states, the average college graduate made 38% more than the average high school graduate. Today, that number is 75% more. More importantly perhaps, is that today's college graduates have a much better chance of passing their legacy down to their children than those who do not go to college. In 1970, college and high school graduates had quite similar lifestyles. Today, the differences in divorce rates, smoking, longevity, obesity, friendship networks and community activism is much greater between the two groups, with the high school graduates being on the downside.

Most of the attention the "Occupy" movements are garnering relates to the "blue" inequalities, but the "red" inequalities may be more important to how we extract ourselves from this economically difficult time. Tens of millions of Americans have and are dropping out of college and high school for many reasons. This is a huge problem because it involves so many citizens. Add to that, 40% of our children are born to unwed mothers, and our workforce of skilled and semi-skilled labor is languishing in dormancy for lack of job opportunities. The key word here is "opportunity".

We might be disgusted at the "blue" inequality of CEO and star athlete salaries compared to everybody else, but the "red" inequality is being saddled with the specter of having no hope. Studies show that poor people have virtually no chance of upward mobility irrespective of their education. The middle classes are showing a steep drop in upward mobility. Subsequent generations do worse than previous ones. Only the educated people coming from already wealthy families are showing any upward trend in socio-economic mobility. The dream of working one's way to the top or out of poverty is dimming rapidly for most Americans.

While corporate America has hastily sent our jobs to other countries, there was no attempt to replace them. While we've let our infrastructure crumble, we've also cut our school vocational programs thus depriving our society of skilled labor resources. We have dumbed down our school curricula for the sake of passing unfunded, but mandated testing regimes that serve no purpose other than political expediency. The children become bored and disinterested and drop out to do any number of things not all of which are legal or productive to society.

I hate to say it, but these trends look an awful lot like what describes a second world nation. Is that what we are, or where we're headed? While the elites scurry to their gated, McMansion communities the vast majority of the working class, the poor and the underclass scrape for a dream of some sort to which they can aspire even as their opportunities to do so dwindle.

There are countless slogans decrying the state we're in and how we've lost our national compass. It was the strong middle class that made this country great. They spent the money and became the engine of our economy. Today, 50 million people live in poverty to varying degrees. They spur nothing. Today, the middle class's job quality and rewards have degraded to a point where they no longer spur the economy either.

Is this where we are headed? If so, how do the elites expect to keep raking in their millions when nobody is making or buying anything other than subsistence?

LESSONS FROM HEROES

The following individuals and groups are heroic to me because they did exceptional things that allowed the progress of modern humans to proceed and flourish as we discovered more about our universe and ourselves. Each are unique in their own ways, but the common thread of heroism for me is that each had a tenacity to do what was right for the most benefits for the most people – whether they knew it or not.

- **St. Thomas Aquinas**: 13th century philosopher and priest; postulated that the universe was created by God when He set the first particle in motion. This is the most elegant, pre-technology hypothesis I know.

- **Albert Einstein:** Famous mathematician and scientist who established Aquinas' hypothesis as the The General and Special Theories of Relativity. He predicted the Big Bang and an expanding universe.

- **Edwin Hubbel:** Proved Einstein's theory by observing galaxies moving away from each other and the Earth "relative" to each other.

- **Jesus Christ:** 1st true liberal. First truly charismatic figure to confront oppression by giving the oppressed faith in their own abilities to rise above and conquer their oppressors, rather than just fight them.

- **Thomas Jefferson & Benjamin Franklin:** First American elites to advocate movement away from elitism as a nation. Their socio-political conflict resolutions were personal and profound: separation of slavery from freedom; church from state; 1st true advocates of education for the masses; first American renaissance men.

- **Gallileo Gallilae:** Validated Copernican theory of the solar system by observing it with his telescope; this early, true science allowed Johannes Kepler to develop orbital theory of planets; proved the church wrong about their theory of the solar system, thus beginning the scientific separation of fact from church dogma.

- **Isaac Newton:** Invented the Calculus and quantified the physics of motion. This laid the basis for extra-terrestrial travel; accurately predicted the mass of the Earth and the velocity of an object needed to escape Earth's gravity.

- **Franklin Delano Roosevelt:** Along with Abraham Lincoln, the most visionary of our Presidents who also finessed difficult social "traditions" to establish new directions for our country. Lincoln dealt with slavery; FDR dealt with the echoes of the civil war and the inherent racism still embedded in society. FDR dealt with anti-semitism all the while the Jews were being persecuted in Germany and elsewhere; Lincoln and FDR were war Presidents during our most trying times; FDR employed Keynesian economic theory and established social services no democracy had ever seen before. FDR wrote and the Congress passed the Glass-Steagall Act which, among other things, prevented Wall St. banks from speculating on markets with depositor money by separating them from deposit banks. His second Bill of Rights, ignored because of the war and his death, illustrated his vision for a truly free and healthy America. They appear in an earlier chapter.

- **Harry Truman:** Rags to President; determined to finish the war and prevent Soviet influence to overwhelm Europe; Lead Senate committee to stop government contract corruption during the war; integrated our armed forces; forced unions and management to reconcile during crucial times; defied a republican Congress to enact extensive labor and anti-trust laws.
- **John F. Kennedy:** The next great visionary for social services and the space program; finessed the Cuban Missile crisis and prevented all-out nuclear war; prepared our exit from Viet Nam.
- **Chuck Yeager:** Test pilot who 1st flew faster than sound; WW II fighter ace who escaped capture to return to flying after being shot down; perfected system preparation and training for USAF test pilot programs; high school graduate.
- **Charles Darwin:** His superb and careful science set the stage for announcing the most important theory ever in the history of life science, Earth science and physical science. The subsequent sciences of biochemistry, genetics and paleontology were either unknown or very new and incompletely understood. His vision, insight and courage helped human understanding of the world leap forward into the development of antibiotics, genetic engineering and the understanding of our places on Earth.
- **Ann Richards:** Overcame alcoholism to become governor of Texas; a caring visionary for people; she considered the Texas people more important than money. We haven't seen anybody nearly like that in Austin since.
- **Alice Randalls:** My high school math teacher; inspirational figure to my teaching career.
- **The Oppressed:** All those who fought and died so that the working classes can have dignity and a chance for a long, healthy life. These are the people who combated capitalistic moguls of the 19th and 20th centuries who were intent on making the workers their indentured servants in working conditions none of us would accept for a second today.
- **The Victims of the Ludlow Massacre:** Symbolic heroes all. The Rockefeller Trust actually paid the salaries of the Colorado National Guard who were ordered to use whatever means to break a labor strike and proceeded to murder women, children and miners who refused to work in intolerable conditions.

Perpetuating the Lie Machine

I had one of those "you've got to be kidding me" moments recently. I read a column by a columnist that said Bill Clinton got a "free pass" for his tryst with Monica Lewinski while the media jumped all over Herman Cain and Supreme Court Justice Clarence Thomas for their "alleged" misdeeds with women and sexual harassment. I guess he forgot that the Clinton/Lewinski affair was consensual. If I'm not mistaken, President Clinton was IMPEACHED by the House of Representatives. Incredibly, even with a significant majority, the Senate couldn't get enough votes to convict President Clinton of perjury...or anything else.

Another piece of whining disinformation in this column was how nearly 50% of our citizens are not paying any taxes while receiving all the largesse our government can dole out. Well, the FACTS are that 90% of that 50% don't make enough money to show up on the tax tables, are working only part-time or are unemployed. The other 10% are paying accountants and lawyers to help them avoid paying taxes at all. The IRS is happy to provide the data for that summation. Oh, and those poor, scruffy, ne'er-do-wells out there expressing their first amendment rights in the occupy movements should be banned from private property because they are disrupting business. Oh dear. Taking a look at the newsreels one sees that there are no businesses being disrupted by the peaceful demonstrations because the great stone buildings where businesses reside on Wall St. and elsewhere are locked. The protesters are NOT interrupting those sacrosanct businesses from continuing the plunder of the middle class.

Another disjointed comment: "power to the people often translates into more power to the government". This is almost true. The problem is that if the government in the United States was allowed to function as it was intended – a government of, by and for the people – we would have nothing to worry about. Instead, beginning in 1971, Lewis Powell, a future Supreme Court Justice appointed by Richard Nixon, called capitalist America to arms. He rallied big business across the nation to create PACs and think tanks and lobbyists all specifically intended to buy the government. Between then and now, lobbying has become as normal to Washington as pigeons on the Mall. So-called think tanks (that only "think" one way: to favor business and finances for the wealthy) now number in the dozens and all are very well endowed by the very people they serve: Wall Street bankers and corporate moguls. This set up used to be called "influence peddling". Now, we call it government by investment.

I have to admit that I'm against a government that is operated like it is run by the stooges of plutocracy. I'm especially prickly about OUR government being operated similarly to the one in Tehran. There they have a board of directors (Mullahs) who pull the strings of a "head of state" so that he puppets what they decide should happen. What passes for a legislature there is just a rubber stamp. In previous columns I've listed in detail the many desires of the American people that have been ignored by their government while other decisions counter to the peoples' desires have made instead.

Our individual freedom begins with believing in a representative government, not scorning government as a method of posturing. Our faith in our nation results from our expecting those we elect to office to do the bidding of the majority, not the monetarily endowed few. To scorn and sneer at those who are doing what they can to make things right peacefully is to identify with elitist principles of an oligarchy that wants to RULE instead of govern. I wonder how those lost liberties will seem then.

This kind of lie packaging is what creates those right wing dictatorships we used to fear and ridicule. Scrambling truth and facts is not just occurring in our schools, it is happening every time we read a paper or watch TV. I have found it very difficult to make sure the passion of beliefs is tempered with the sober facts and reality in the context of real, unabridged history. Knowing and understanding history tends to prevent us from repeating the mistakes that made us less great.

Supporting Data

For most of this book you have been reading my opinions based on my research of facts and news. I have tried my best to be as objective as possible. The section below is corroboration I discovered AFTER I wrote this manuscript. I thought it would help you, the reader, see validity in my sense of urgency and ideas for turning the national momentum around as this author encourages and suggests.

The following are excerpts taken from an article written by G. William Domhoff, Professor at the University of California at Santa Cruz about our wealth and income distribution. Although the professor is inclined toward a liberal viewpoint, he does present objective data and conclusions. He is very much on point by not revealing a preference toward either political faction, but clearly demonstrates the economic schism that has emerged over the past decade; thus giving some degree of credence to the Occupy Wall Street demonstrators.

The surge in the population of baby boomers, never before witnessed or at least quantified in modern history, has obviated a significant income increase for this group currently representing the vast majority of earners at the peak of their careers. Also, this age segment now and always has earned predominately in the top 20% of the income strata. Of note is the surge in the wealth and income gap during the Clinton years, reduced slightly during the Bush II years.

Table 1: **Distribution of income in the United States, 1982-2006**

| | Income | | |
	Top 1 percent	Next 19 percent	Bottom 80 percent
1982	12.8%	39.1%	48.1%
1988	16.6%	38.9%	44.5%
1991	15.7%	40.7%	43.7%
1994	14.4%	40.8%	44.9%
1997	16.6%	39.6%	43.8%
2000	20.0%	38.7%	41.4%
2003	17.0%	40.8%	42.2%
2006	21.3%	40.1%	38.6%

We can still safely say that the top 10% of the world's adults control about 85% of global household wealth -- defined very broadly as all assets (not just financial assets), minus debts. That compares with a figure of 69.8% for the top 10% for the United States.

Figure 1: **Share of wealth held by the Bottom 99% and Top 1% in the United States, 1922-**

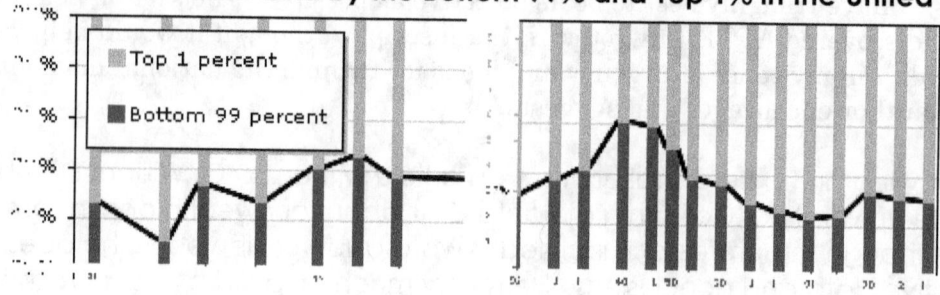

2007.

This chart demonstrates clearly that the wealth distribution in the US, and most other countries for that matter, has in modern times more or less always been as it is today.

The rate of increase is even higher for the very richest of the rich: the top 400 income earners in the United States. According to another analysis by Johnston, the average income of the top 400 tripled during the Clinton Administration and doubled during the first seven years of the Bush Administration.

The impact of "transfer payments"

As we've seen, taxes don't have much impact on the income distribution, especially when we look at the top 1% or top 0.1%. Nor do various kinds of tax breaks and loopholes have much impact on the income distribution overall. That's because the tax deductions that help those with lower incomes -- such as the Earned Income Tax Credit (EITC), tax forgiveness for low-income earners on Social Security, and tax deductions for dependent children -- are offset by the breaks for high-income earners (for example: dividends and capital gains are only taxed at a rate of 15%; there's no tax on the interest earned from state and municipal bonds; and 20% of the tax deductions taken for dependent children actually go to people earning over $100,000 a year).

It is sometimes said that income inequality is reduced significantly by government programs that matter very much in the lives of low-income Americans. These programs provide "transfer payments," which are a form of income for those in need. They include unemployment compensation, cash payments to the elderly who don't have enough to live on from Social Security, Temporary Assistance to Needy Families (welfare), food stamps, and Medicaid.

Thomas Hungerford (2009), a tax expert who works for the federal government's Congressional Research Service, carried out a study for Congress that tells us about the real-world impact of transfer payments on reducing income inequality. Hungerford's study is based on 2004 income data from an ongoing study of a representative sample of families at the University of Michigan, and it includes the effects of both taxes and four types of transfer payments (Social Security, Temporary Assistance to Needy Families, food stamps, and Medicaid). The table that follows shows the income inequality index (that is, the Gini coefficient) at three points along the way: (1.) before taxes or transfers; (2) after taxes are taken into account; and (3) after both taxes and transfer payments are included in the equation.

Table 2: **Redistributive effect of taxes and transfer payments**

Income definition	Gini index
Before taxes and transfers	0.5116
After taxes, before transfers	0.4774
After taxes and transfers	0.4284

Source: Congressional Research Service, adapted from Hungerford (2009).

As seen here, Hungerford's findings first support what we had learned earlier from the Citizens for Tax Justice study: taxes don't do much to reduce inequality. They secondly reveal that transfer payments have a *slightly* larger impact on inequality than taxes, but not much. Third, his findings tell us that taxes and transfer payments together reduce the inequality index from .52 to .43, which is very close to the CIA's estimate of .45 for 2008.

In short, for those who ask if progressive taxes and transfer payments even things out to a significant degree, the answer is that while they have some effect, they don't do nearly as much in our country as they do in Canada, major European countries, or Japan.

My comment (Domhoff): **"The following is a serious development I have personally witnessed within the most powerful segment of our society- the corporate/government alliance, resulting in what can be euphemistically termed "Executive Featherbedding". This practice has evolved clearly by design, and can be arrested only by our government officials in all 3 branches.** *The trouble for our system of government is the blatant abuse of position, both from the corporate and government sectors, allowing this partnership to thrive* **(Italics mine). Government contractors, voting themselves on** their boards, approving outlandish compensation packages, and crossing over frequently between their private business positions to lucrative ongoing government positions, either as elected officials or hired "consultants", possessing the most tyrannical power over policies and laws, have permeated and petrified in our societal decision-making faction so deeply that our current political election process has been relegated to complete impotence. "

Income Ratios and Power: Executives vs. Laborers

Another way that income can be used as a power indicator is by comparing average CEO annual pay to average factory worker pay, something that has been done for many years by *Business Week* and, later, the Associated Press. The ratio of CEO pay to factory worker pay rose from 42:1 in 1960 to as high as 531:1 in 2000, at the height of the stock market bubble, when CEOs were cashing in big stock options. It was at 411:1 in 2005 and 344:1 in 2007, according to research by United for a Fair Economy. By way of comparison, the same ratio is about 25:1 in Europe. The changes in the American ratio from 1960 to 2007 are displayed in Figure 2, which is based on data from several hundred of the largest corporations.

Figure 2: **CEOs' pay as a multiple of the average worker's pay, 1960-2007**

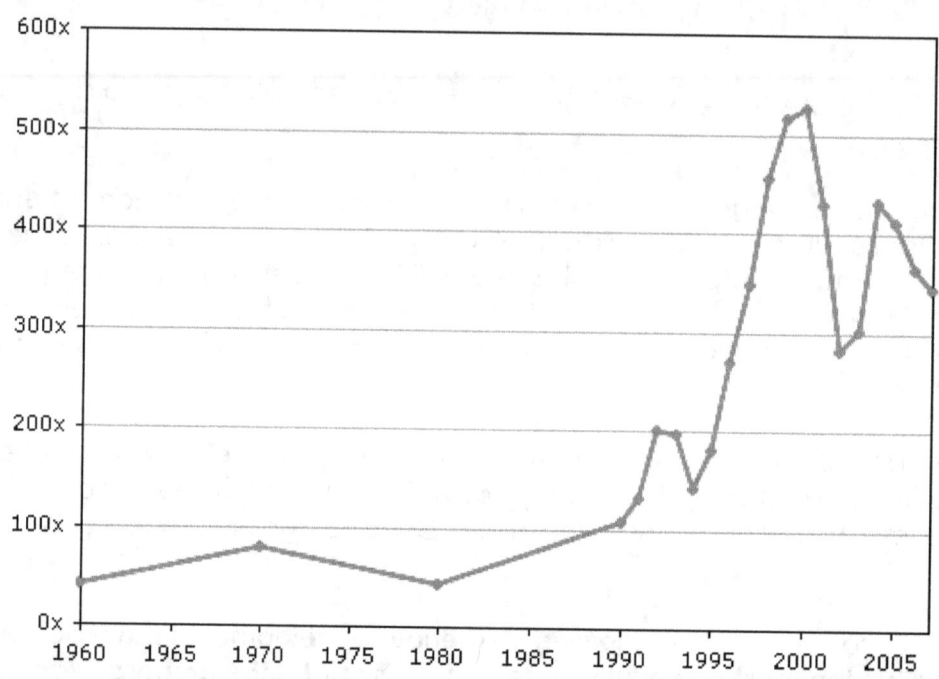

Source: *Executive Excess 2008*, the 15th Annual CEO Compensation Survey from the Institute for Policy Studies and United for a Fair Economy.

It's even more revealing to compare the actual rates of increase of the salaries of CEOs and ordinary workers; from 1990 to 2005, CEOs' pay increased almost 300% (adjusted for inflation), while production workers gained a scant 4.3%. The purchasing power of the federal minimum wage actually *declined* by 9.3% when inflation is taken into account. These startling results are illustrated in Figure 3.

Figure 3: **CEOs' average pay, production workers' average pay, the S&P 500 Index, corporate profits, and the federal minimum wage, 1990-2005 (all figures adjusted for inflation)**

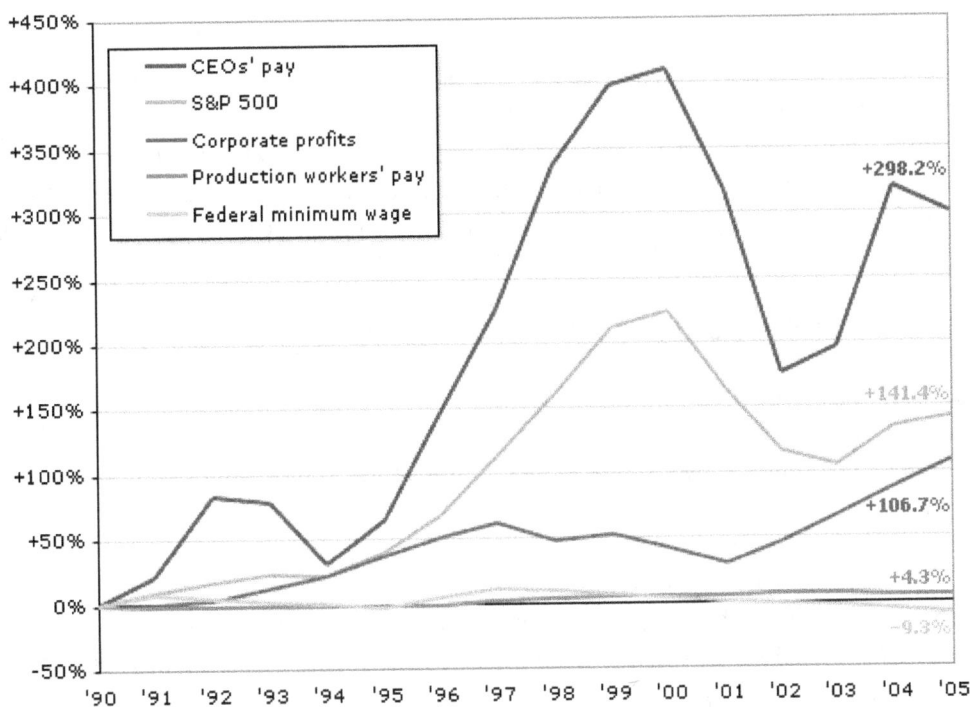

Source: *Executive Excess 2006*, the 13th Annual CEO Compensation Survey from the Institute for Policy Studies and United for a Fair Economy.

Although some of the information I've relied upon to create this section on executives' vs. workers' pay is a few years old now, the AFL/CIO provides up-to-date information on CEO salaries at their Web site. There, you can learn that the median compensation for CEO's in *all* industries as of early 2010 is $3.9 million; it's $10.6 million for the companies listed in Standard and Poor's 500, and $19.8 million for the companies listed in the Dow-Jones Industrial Average. Since the median worker's pay is about $36,000, then you can quickly calculate that CEOs in general make 100 times as much as the workers, that CEO's of S&P 500 firms make almost 300 times as much, and that CEOs at the Dow-Jones companies make 550 times as much. (For a more recent update on CEOs' pay, see "The Drought Is Over (At Least for CEOs)" at NYTimes.com; the article reports that the median compensation for CEOs at 200 major companies was $9.6 million in 2010 -- up by about 12% over 2009 and generally equal to or surpassing pre-recession levels. For specific information about some of the top CEOs, see http://projects.nytimes.com/executive_compensation.

If you wonder how such a large gap could develop, the most immediate factor involves the way in which CEOs are now able to rig things so that the board of directors, which they help select -- and which includes some fellow CEOs on whose boards they sit -- gives them the pay they want. The trick is in hiring outside experts, called "compensation consultants," who give the process a thin veneer of economic respectability.

The process has been explained in detail by a retired CEO of DuPont, Edgar S. Woolard, Jr., who is now chair of the New York Stock Exchange's executive compensation committee. His experience suggests that he knows whereof he speaks, and he speaks because he's concerned that corporate leaders are losing respect in the public mind. He says that the business page chatter about CEO salaries being set by the competition for their services in the executive labor market is "bull." As to the claim that CEOs deserve ever higher salaries because they "create wealth," he describes that rationale as a "joke," says the New York Times (Morgenson, 2005).

Here's how it works, according to Woolard:

The compensation committee [of the board of directors] talks to an outside consultant who has surveys you could drive a truck through and pay anything you want to pay, to be perfectly honest. The outside consultant talks to the human resources vice president, who talks to the CEO. The CEO says what he'd like to receive. It gets to the human resources person who tells the outside consultant. And it pretty well works out that the CEO gets what he's implied he thinks he deserves, so he will be respected by his peers. (Morgenson, 2005.)

The board of directors buys into what the CEO asks for because the outside consultant is an "expert" on such matters. Furthermore, handing out only modest salary increases might give the wrong impression about how highly the board values the CEO. And if someone on the board should object, there are the three or four CEOs from other companies who will make sure it happens. It is a process with a built-in escalator.

As for why the consultants go along with this scam, they know which side their bread is buttered on. They realize the CEO has a big say-so on whether or not they are hired again. So they suggest a package of salaries, stock options and other goodies that they think will please the CEO, and they, too, get rich in the process. And certainly the top executives just below the CEO don't mind hearing about the boss's raise. They know it will mean pay increases for them, too. (For an excellent detailed article on the main consulting firm that helps CEOs and other corporate executives raise their pay, check out the New York Times article entitled "America's Corporate Pay Pal", which supports everything Woolard of DuPont claims and adds new information.)

If hiring a consulting firm doesn't do the trick as far as raising CEO pay, then it may be possible for the CEO to have the board change the way in which the success of the company is determined. For example, Walmart Stores, Inc. used to link the CEO's salary to sales figures at established stores. But when declining sales no longer led to big pay raises, the board simply changed the magic formula to use total companywide sales instead. By that measure, the CEO could still receive a pay hike (Morgenson, 2011).

There's a much deeper power story that underlies the self-dealing and mutual back-scratching by CEOs now carried out through interlocking directorates and seemingly independent outside consultants. It probably involves several factors. At the least, on the workers' side, it reflects their loss of power following the all-out attack on unions in the 1960s and 1970s, which is explained in detail in an excellent book by James Gross (1995), a labor and industrial relations professor at Cornell. That decline in union power made possible and was increased by both outsourcing at home and the movement of production to developing countries, which were facilitated by the break-up of the New Deal coalition and the rise of the New Right (Domhoff, 1990, Chapter 10). It signals the shift of the United States from a high-wage to a low-wage economy, with professionals protected by the fact that foreign-trained doctors and lawyers aren't allowed to compete with their American counterparts in the direct way that low-wage foreign-born workers are.

On the other side of the class divide, the rise in CEO pay may reflect the increasing power of chief executives as compared to major owners and stockholders in general, not just their increasing power over workers. CEOs may now be the center of gravity in the corporate community and the power elite, displacing the leaders in wealthy owning families (e.g., the second and third generations of the Walton family, the owners of Wal-Mart). True enough, the CEOs are sometimes ousted by their generally go-along boards of directors, but they are able to make hay and throw their weight around during the time they are king of the mountain.

The claims made in the previous paragraph need much further investigation, but they demonstrate the ideas and research directions that are suggested by looking at the wealth and income distributions as indicators of power.

My final comment (Domhoff): *Suffice it to say, our system of government has truly been captivated by the most severely corrupt citizenry ever assembled in our relatively short history as a nation* (Italics mine). The sad reality is that we as "average Americans" consistently trudge through our lives, supporting our families, striving to be honest in all our relationships, and demonstrating clearly that we are truly the most generous society to have emerged from human evolution. We give more to each other, to charitable organizations, to other countries, both ongoing and in times of disaster. I for one, enjoy what I have been so graciously privileged to experience, in my work, social life, and family life. The freedoms we have in this country are unequaled, now and across the walls of time. However, this freedom is subtly being compromised right under our noses, and the trend is rapidly on an accelerating pace. Our children and grandchildren will not be able to push our tragic crises forward any longer. Our demise does not have to be! We are spoiled rotten from the sense of complacency with the demand for true and honest leadership. But we as a people must take the burden of leading the country. It unfortunately won't be through our conventional political process, but through a change promulgated by demonstration to a degree that other countries are now experiencing. The difference is fortunately not a demonstration for a change in the system, but a change in leadership. We must as a people insist with action that the attributes of sacrifice and honesty be the characteristics of all our officials, both corporate and government. Money is really not the issue; but the catalyst that has been used by those born within or smarter than most to extend their obsessive greed and lust for power and comfort. Some may call it a "spiritual" disease. We must carry our demands for a psychic change through those now in power, or take decisive actions to remove those through our election process or other means. The demonstrations of the 60's influenced major moral changes not in policies but leadership behavior!

AFTERWORD

The subject matter in this book is serious stuff, to be sure. The trick in closing this book is to leave you, the reader, with a somewhat hopeful and positive attitude that you can take with you in your pursuit of action and search for truth. My wife counseled me that there needed to be some constructive ideas included. I have done that in some of the chapters, but those are just *my* ideas, not yours.

The current economic and social situations here in the United States of America, if allowed to continue, will certainly create the kind of chaos and insecurity of life that third world countries experience on a daily basis. We have a window of opportunity to avoid those wracking upheavals, but we must act quickly. Taken by itself, it doesn't matter that we demonstrate in the streets our displeasure to the powers that be. What matters is that we motivate others who are witnessing our activism to demonstrate their own, personal activism.

From the news reports of the "Occupy" movements being disparaged, demonized and otherwise vilified by the so-called establishment, it is clear that they are frightened and concerned. The great theft of wealth may be over for those operatives and they don't seem to like that. Don't misunderstand: I have nothing against people becoming wealthy. I do NOT believe in communism. I WANT people to get rich! I want a LOT of people to get rich. If a lot of people are getting rich that means something in our economy and national fabric is creating that wealth.

That something is LABOR. WORK. Jobs that pay a living wage, programs that train people to be ABLE to earn those wages, innovation from new businesses that create demand for that labor are the things needed to make all those new millionaires. The best part is that this reinvigorated workforce will regenerate the middle class which will start consuming again and thus drive our economy back to its levels of egalitarian excellence. There is NO reason, for example, for those CEOs to earn 500 times more than their factory workers. In Europe it's only 25 times, an entire order of magnitude! It surely begs the question: How much money does one person really need to lead a life in the American Dream?

I once did an exercise with my students about wealth and what we can spend it on. At the time Tiger Woods was the athlete who was most famous and made more money than any other. We picked the year when he grossed $100 million. Each student was asked to imagine themselves with absolutely nothing: no clothes, no house, no car....nothing except $100 million. We decided to pay our 35% income tax first. O.K. After buying 3 changes of clothes for every day of the year, a Bentley automobile equivalent for every day of the week, a 20,000 square foot mansion in the U.S. and another, smaller, but lavishly furnished villa on the Costa del Sol in Spain, a kitchen staff, all new furniture, three wonderful meals a day, jewelry, a Gulfstream jet and a 100 foot yacht with crew, pilots, drivers and business managers we were left with about $11 million walking around money. After a long pause, I asked them what they would spend next year's net income on. They got the point.

Finally, I would like to pull a Lewis Powell in reverse. I would like to call to "arms" my fellow Americans to return control of the government of the United States to us, the non-corporate mogul, the non-super rich bond trader, the non-hedge fund billionaire, the non-bankers of Wall Street. First of all, we have to realize how badly we screwed up by allowing these Powell-originated power mongers to gain control of our government by bribes and other nefarious means including influencing the U.S. Supreme Court. That realization, then, must create the motive to do, as Mr. Domhoff says, what is necessary to place our government into the hands of those representatives who actually believe in and *walk the walk* of government of, by and for the *people.*

Make no mistake. We are in a fight for our very existence as a nation, or at least the nation our founders tried to establish. They did not create a nation for capitalists to rule. They created a nation for *We the people...* to govern. Jefferson and Washington feared capitalists. I refuse to rise to the bait of convenient label plastering on this attitude. This is what our founders intended. They said so. Millions of our citizens have paid the ultimate sacrifice to defend those words and the words of our Constitution and the Declaration of Independence. Many more have died trying to engender fairness, safety and dignity in the lives of working men and women. It is my desire that their deaths and sacrifices were not in vain.

I choose to not be a lackey of Wall St. or any other street. I choose to not be a slave to oppressive and excessive wealth and the power implied. I refuse to let my government and thus my country revert to a medieval form of *Lords vs. Serfs* government. We didn't become great by doing so and we cannot return to greatness as a nation and a beacon for mankind by allowing those would-be lords have their way with us. WE have the vote. WE have the voices and WE have the numbers to assure our nation's righteous moral compass and secure the civic actions that are necessary to leap beyond mere economic power and aspire to our imagination that only our dreams can create.

Only we can decide what the dream of democracy will look like in the near and long-term future.

ACKNOWLEDGEMENTS

There are many people who have influenced my writing "career", as well as helping provide an intellectually vibrant atmosphere that allows me to research, create and write my ideas. My editor at *The River Cities Daily Tribune* has been most encouraging and supportive. The day he told me that he's been looking for someone like me to write for his op-ed page melted any resistance and fatigue I had from doing so that first year.

My very good friends Conrad Vernon and Charlie Vincent have kept me informed and engaged in those issues we all hold dear to our beings. Without their support and inputs, my articles would be less than they are.

Among my progressive and "liberal" friends I have to include Kathleen To, Cristi Clements, Jo Tedder, the Guinns, Kathy Carvell, Bob Suhocki, Jason Lillegraven, Jim Denton, Chris Akins, Steve Love, Sunshine Williams and Jerry Garvin. These folks have commented and critiqued my work for two years and homage must be paid to their patience and perseverance.

I owe special tribute to my soul mate without portfolio, Ms. Molly Wingate. She has kept me inspired and interested in a variety of things, issues and the approaches to writing that I only imagined. We've critiqued each others' works and have been made better for it. I don't know how it could be any better than that.

Finally, I want to pay tribute to those people who are enduring today what my generation endured in the 60s and 70s to foment social and moral change in our country. Those people demonstrating against the whole package of misdeeds and unfair practices in the "Occupy" movements have my eternal respect and support. Complex issue reform requires constant, but patient energy and dedication. My thoughts are with those who see what I see and who have the strength, youth and vigor to do what I cannot to fix what is broken and return our government to those who actually mean to govern not rule.

V.M.T.